Learn to
Fly-cast
in a weekend

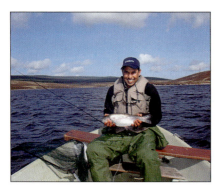

Learn to Fly-cast
in a weekend

Tim Rolston

Published by Struik Publishers (a division of New Holland Publishing (South Africa) (Pty) Ltd)
New Holland Publishing is a member of Johnnic Communications Ltd
Cornelis Struik House, 80 McKenzie Street, Cape Town 8001
86 Edgware Road, London, W2 2EA, United Kingdom
Unit 1, 66 Gibbes Street, Chatswood, NSW 2067, Australia
218 Lake Road, Northcote, Auckland, New Zealand

www.struik.co.za

Publishing manager: Linda de Villiers
Managing editor: Cecilia Barfield
Editor: Anthony Sharpe
Designer: Helen Henn

Reproduction: Hirt & Carter Cape (Pty) Ltd
Printing and binding: Craft Print International Ltd.

Photographic credits: Top photo page 2, main photo page 3, Sudesh Pursad

ISBN 978-1-77007-440-8

10 9 8 7 6 5 4 3 2 1

www.imagesofafrica.co.za

IMAGES OF AFRICA
PHOTO LIBRARY

Over 40 000 unique African images available to purchase from our image bank at www.imagesofafrica.co.za

Acknowledgements:

Putting together an instructional book such as this makes demands on a lot more people than just the author. Of the many who have been of valuable assistance and provided much-needed encouragement and support I would like to thank in particular:

Gordon McKay, without whom this adventure to better understand and teach fly-casting would never have even started.

Debbie Marshbank, who served as photographer for many of the images used in this book, and provided endless support for the project.

David Levine of Stealth Fly Rod and Reel, for his determined support and sponsorship of the South African National Fly-fishing Team and for much of the tackle photographed in this publication.

Tony Short and David Edkins, the most wonderful gentlemen and clients who not only re-awakened in me the pure joy of fly-fishing, but who proved once and for all that the methods illustrated in this book really do work, and encouraged me to put them all down on paper so that other anglers might benefit from them.

The Struik team: Anthony Sharpe, my editor, who underwent a crash course in fly-casting and did a great deal of polishing of the manuscript, such that hopefully the readers will gain the most from its content. Helen Henn, for putting it all together in the clearest and most attractive format possible. Linda de Villiers, for showing faith in a first-time author.

Finally, I would like to thank all those anglers with whom I have been fortunate enough to cross paths and waterways at some point or another. Fly-fishing is an endlessly complicated and involved pursuit; it is simply not possible to become proficient at it without the assistance and encouragement of others, and as a group, fly-fishermen in general seem to be an inordinately helpful lot. Much of what I have learned over the years and hope to continue to learn comes from the passing of knowledge and experience from one angler to another. People have willingly shared their experiences, experiments and failures with remarkable enthusiasm, and it is this willingness to assist others that binds together fly-fishermen from all over the world and serves to make our chosen sport what it is.

My sincere thanks to you all and I trust that none of us have quite finished learning yet, because so much of the joy of fly-fishing is linked to the endless pursuit of knowledge and a better understanding of our passion.

Contents

In the beginning

Gordon and I had slipped away from work and the madding crowd of the city to spend a long mid-week break far up in the mountains on one of the most beautiful trout streams you could ever imagine. In those days there was little by way of a path, and what there was criss-crossed the stream over and over again, making for a long and strenuous hike into this remote spot. The effort was well worth it though; the water really was as clear as gin and the remoteness of the spot served as its own protection against over-fishing and pollution, with the result that the quality of the fishing was exceeded only by the scenic beauty and tranquillity of the place.

We had hiked and fished with our packs on our backs for the first day, a cumbersome if necessary evil that allowed us to sleep under the stars for a night or two and venture even higher up the gorge in search of more remote spots and hopefully even larger trout. The stream was renowned not only for the clarity of the water and the remoteness of the venue (a serious accident up here could easily prove to be fatal), but also because it produced some incredibly large fish on occasion.

It was our last day on the river and with a long, arduous hike ahead of us and absolutely no possibility of managing the march in the dark, we were under some pressure to call it a day and head homewards. We had caught lots of fish, large and small, stalking them in the clear water, and camped a few nights on the riverbank under a large overhang that afforded some measure of comfort, if not actual luxury. By most standards we enjoyed

The author with a fish taken by accurate casting on a crystal clear Cape stream.

a superb expedition, but when such trips are *that* good and the next chance to be on such waters is *that* far away one feels that one should make the most of things. Although the sun was dropping lower on the horizon and we were beginning to envision a forced march (if not a run!) down the mountain, we decided to try just one final pool before turning tail.

This particular spot we always refer to as 'Emerald Pool' as the water, despite its clarity, has such depth at this point in the river that it appears the most gorgeous deep green colour. It also represents the last fishable spot on the river accessible without serious mountaineering and holds large numbers of good-sized fish too. It was a traditional 'last cast' spot and, with the waterfall at the head of the run, ferns growing out of the rocks and overhanging trees covered in ancient moss, made a fitting place to say good-bye to the stream for another season.

Beautiful yellowfish water on the Orange River. Whilst long casts are not necessary in such rapid water, line control is critical to success.

It was Gordon's turn to fish. We always take it in turns on these streams; it makes for a fun way to fish, at the same time avoiding competition amongst the anglers and unnecessary disturbance of the stream (which would undoubtedly result in a lot of spooked fish). There was a good-looking fish sipping in small spinners in the middle reaches of the pool, but it was too deep to wade closer and the sheer rock faces on either side prevented an alternative approach other than casting from the tail out. Furthermore, the overhanging yellowwood tree didn't give much room for a back cast. It is a spectacular pool to be sure but one that is rather tricky to fish given the geography of its surroundings.

Gordon lengthened his line with a couple of false casts, geared up for the final delivery of the fly and promptly hooked the overhanging yellowwood behind him. Having unhitched the fly he made a second cast that fell short, well behind the fish, and when lengthening his line he once more caught up in the tree to his rear. Two more attempts to cover the elusive and still-feeding fish resulted in the exact same confrontation with the vegetation and Gordon declared the fish out of range and uncatchable. He did, however, have the good grace to declare that I was more than welcome to have a go at what was now becoming a sought-after prize.

I made two false casts, shot a heap of line on the final forward stroke and landed the fly just ahead of the fish, which promptly turned slightly to its right and inhaled the imitation. At the end of a spirited fight the fish was netted and carefully returned to the water

whereupon Gordon said simply: 'How the hell did you reach that fish with the tree in the way?' It was one of the first of many lessons on the advantages of being able to cast well. That fish was surely out of reach of anyone not able to generate lots of line speed with a short cast, and then shoot additional line on the final delivery to reach the fish.

Sometimes it doesn't seem to matter that much, but often enough good casting means the difference between success and failure. Being able to cast well is not all about catching more fish but it is about being as effective as possible, and at the same time enjoying the experience of fly-fishing more as a result.

A visiting angler makes short, accurate casts into pocket water on the Molenaars River in the Western Cape.

Both casting distance and accuracy greatly increase the angler's chances of success on clear stillwaters like this one near Barrydale.

I don't think Gordon ever quite forgave me for catching 'his' fish, but the experience did lead us both into a careful examination of fly-casting and a long period of experimentation and improvement of our abilities, to the point that I rarely think about casting whilst I am fishing any more (although I do still practise on occasion).

This book is all about making you a better caster. Whether you are casting tiny dries on light lines to spooky trout in a spring creek, or belting out massive poppers to marauding King Fish in the surf, good technique will save you a lot of frustration, sore arms, tangled lines and lost flies. It may even improve your catch rate as well. At the end of the day being able to cast well will enhance both the efficacy and enjoyment of your fishing. Better casting is not an end in itself, but it is the stepping-stone to better angling and more fun.

So, enjoy the process detailed in this book and you will emerge a better caster and angler. Good anglers cast well, and once you have mastered casting you can move on to worrying about all the other important stuff, like catching more fish.

Introduction

Fly-fishing is supposed to be fun, it is supposed to be pleasurable and bring you joy and peace. However, if you are going to enjoy it that means that you are going to have to cast with fly-fishing gear. Now despite the fact that many would have us believe that fly-casting is a feat mastered only by contortionists and certified sword-swallowers, the reality is that learning to cast a fly is no more tricky than learning to drive a car, kick a rugby ball or swing a golf club, in fact it's probably a whole lot easier. The aim of this book is to provide a simple, logical and concise guide to improving your casting FOREVER. There are explanations as to why this system works but if you wish you can just follow the exercises without the technical stuff and still progress rapidly to the point where your casting needs little if any thought.

The techniques and exercises in this book are primarily the result of research and experimentation undertaken by myself and my very good friend Gordon McKay. At the time of starting this research we were, like so many fly-fishermen, not entirely happy with our own skills. Although many would probably have considered us to be good casters, we felt that we could improve and set about rebuilding our fly-casting techniques from scratch. We did a great deal of research, including reading books by Charles Ritz, Lefty Kreh, Joan Wulff and others, all famed for their casting tuition. This led to three interesting discoveries.

Firstly, we found that much of what has been written and discussed relating to fly-casting technique is, in our opinion, erroneous. Secondly, we found ourselves in the unfortunate position of having to 'unlearn' what we already knew so as to improve, a common problem for many people, even those who have been fly-fishing for a number of years. Thirdly, and perhaps the biggest breakthrough, was the realisation that, having worked out how to cast fly-tackle effectively, we needed to come up with a means of transferring that knowledge to others in the most effective manner possible. It was this desire to be able to teach others that led to the development of the exercises demonstrated in this book, methods that have already been used to turn hundreds of neophytic anglers into exceptional casters.

Extensive study of a variety of literature, tutorial books and tapes revealed to us that not all good fly-casters are good tutors of fly-casting, and not all tutors of fly-casting actually understand what is going on when they cast. In fact, on more than one occasion we have seen various fly-casting instructors do something completely different from that which they recommend to their clients. The only explanation for this would seem to be that they don't really know what it is that they do when they are casting. Whilst this is entirely acceptable for an angler, we feel it is not so for an instructor.

In this book you will find basic exercises that allow us to break up the casting stroke into simple smaller components. Mastery of each component in turn will build into perfect casting in no time at all. Some people will certainly find one exercise easier than another but the methods highlighted in this book have been used to teach hundreds of people to cast well. The system has worked for anglers of all walks of life – men and women, young and old – and there is absolutely no reason why it won't work for you. In fact, I am prepared to guarantee that it will.

It is worth mentioning early on that this book is not intended to be a comprehensive guide to fly-fishing. Although we have included some basic information on what kinds of gear to buy and their various applications, the book does not discuss the nuances of actual fishing such as fly types, presentation, playing and striking the fish, etc. To include, in addition to the fly-casting instructions, technical information on the myriad fly-fishing techniques out there is simply beyond the scope of a single publication but perhaps will indeed offer the opportunity for a further title in the future.

This book is intended rather as a guide to perfecting the foundation of fly-fishing: the cast. Having mastered this foundation you will be free to explore all the possibilities that fly-fishing can afford you without hindrance or frustration and gain maximum enjoyment in whatever direction your fly-fishing passions may take you.

So enjoy the process, learn to cast and then get out there and enjoy your fishing. Whilst you can undoubtedly impress your friends as well with your newfound ability, the important point is that from here on the days when you are secretly frustrated or embarrassed by your casting are about to come to an end. Those fish on the edge of the weed beds or under the trees will suddenly be in range, the wind will no longer force you to pack in and head home, and you will get fewer tangles, lose fewer flies, catch more fish and have more fun.

The author with a juvenile largemouth yellowfish, taken whilst fishing nymphs on the Orange River.

Why is fly-casting 'different'?

This may seem like a fundamental point to make, but fly-casting is most certainly quite different from almost any other form of casting used in any of a wide variety of fishing styles and techniques. It is not as though someone came along and decided to make things difficult for everyone for no apparent reason. The reality is that, for the most part, fly-fishing requires casting a 'fly' or lure that has next to no mass at all and is far too light to be simply thrown any significant distance. Whilst these days there certainly are large and even some heavy fly-patterns, the basic truth remains: flies don't weigh much. It may be a simple matter to fling half a sardine and a four-ounce sinker into the middle distance, but the same is not true of a size 22 dry fly with the mass of an anorexic gnat.

Originally, there was actually no attempt made to cast flies any distance at all. They were merely lowered onto the water, the angler having snuck up close enough to the fish to allow such a manoeuvre. This style is referred to as 'dapping', but it is obviously very limiting.

Distance isn't everything – fast and accurate casting with a short line are demanding skills, but essential to success on fast pocket water like this section of the Elandspad in the Western Cape.

Improved casting technique can increase one's confidence on large rivers, where distance casting is often required for success.

Thankfully, someone eventually came up with the bright idea of putting the weight into the line instead of the lure.

This is the fundamental difference between fly-casting and any other form of casting: simply that the weight is in a different place and consequentially the means of throwing it any distance is different too. So in fly-casting it is essential to understand that *you are casting the line and not the fly on the end*; the fly simply 'goes along for the ride'.

Though the mass is in the line, one cannot, however, simply pick up a bunch of line and throw it at the fish. The ratio of surface area to mass would result in the entire lot landing not a long way from your feet in a nasty and tangled heap. Hence, the technique of fly-casting developed.

As you may well expect, because the casting style is quite different it stands to reason that fly-fishing tackle is also very different to other types of fishing gear. In the next section we are going to have a brief look at fly-fishing tackle, just enough so that you can recognise the important bits and start off on the right footing with properly configured gear.

Understanding fly-fishing equipment

Some of you may be very familiar with fly-fishing equipment, whilst the complete novices probably are not. The purpose of this section is not to offer a comprehensive discussion of all the variations of fly-fishing gear, but rather to provide some basic explanations so that the novice can better understand why fly-casting looks and works the way it does, and what equipment you will need to practise casting and start fishing.

The best source of quality advice on fishing tackle for the type of fishing you wish to do, and the area in which you plan to fish, is your local specialist fly-fishing outfitter. Novices should always go to a specialist shop; you may pay a little more money but the advice that you receive will save you far more in the long run. Most fly-shops are run by people who are passionate about fly-fishing, and they will be very happy to offer all manner of advice that should assist you greatly in terms of selecting the correct tackle.

The BIG difference

Fly-fishing is, for the most part (although not always completely), about casting flies, whether imitations of insects or frogs or baitfish, all of which weigh very little indeed. In fact, when it comes to fly-casting, it is better to assume that the fly has no weight at all, and to be honest it is trickier to cast if it does. So, in fly-casting *the weight is in the line*.

Whether the fly-line is designed to float, sink, lie just underneath the surface film or whatever, its primary purpose is to provide the necessary mass to be able to cast it and take the fly along for the ride at the same time. You may well have noticed that fly-lines, or at least the boxes they come in, have 'weights' on them, the 'AFTMA' (American Fishing Tackle Manufacturers Association) number. We will discuss this more later on, but for now let's say that the AFTMA number represents the 'weight' of the line, and therefore provides an indication of the rod for which it is best suited.

Fly-lines

For the novice angler the price of a fly-line may seem absurd, but the line is a complex and carefully engineered piece of equipment. Furthermore, if used and cared for properly it will offer you years of use. The fly-line is a critical part of the tackle as a whole, so don't skimp on the line and don't use one not 'matched' to the weight rating of the rod. Mismatched tackle can make learning to fly-cast a tricky proposition for anyone, and you don't want to start off on the wrong foot.

So, the reason fly-casting is so different to the casting in other forms of fishing is simply that we are not casting a distinct mass as one would with a lead weight. Instead, we are casting the mass of the line, which is not in a discrete package, and to complicate things further its mass changes depending on how far we cast it. Essentially, the more line in the air the heavier it is. You should see then that the mass of the line is critically important and it must match the rod with which you use it.

There are a myriad different bits of fly-fishing equipment, but you will be able to cast with any matched outfit.

Today it is fairly simple to get the right combination, as a reputable specialist fly-fishing tackle store will match it up for you. In simple terms: all rods now have a number on them called the AFTMA number, and all lines have the same. Pick a line with the same number as the rod and the combination should work well enough. There is a lot of debate around this subject and one can get very technical about it, but for the novice, pick a line that matches the rod and get on with fishing.

For the purpose of the exercises in this book it will be far easier if you use a floating fly-line, preferably of a bright colour so that you can see it in the air whilst you are practising. Whilst learning to fly-cast it matters little what line and rod weight you use as long as they match. AFTMA #5 or #6 is probably ideal for the beginner but you can use any other matched setup and still achieve perfect results. **Suitable line weights of rods and lines for different types of fishing can be found at the back of this book.**

You will also find that there are hundreds of different lines out there with differing tapers: weight forward lines, double taper lines, rocket taper lines, etc. You can learn to cast with any of them, although a brightly coloured or at least light-coloured floating line is recommended for practising. This will allow you to see the line in the air, something that is quite important when you are learning.

Adding a leader

The leader is the nylon line at the end of the fly-line to which the fly or flies are attached when fishing. In England (and the English can often over-complicate things) this is still sometimes confusingly referred to as a 'cast', but pay them no heed as they are talking about what everybody else refers to as a leader.

For the purposes of the exercises in this book you need only add a length of level monofilament line; any nylon with a breaking

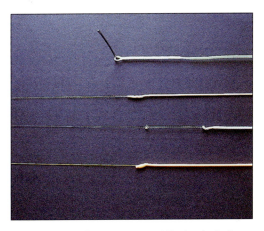

There are lots of ways to connect the leader to the fly-line, but for the purposes of learning to cast any of them will do just fine.

strain from about 3 kg to 5 kg will suffice. When you are actually fishing, the leader becomes a lot more important and we could discuss it for hours, but for now stick on some level monofilament and get on with things.

The simple fact is that you don't want to be wasting money destroying expensive tapered leaders when you are simply practising the casting stroke. If your fly-shop has fitted a leader for you, take it off and add straight nylon monofilament to the end of the

All fly-rods and fly-line packaging now have AFTMA numbers on them, making it very simple to select gear that is designed to work properly together as a unit.

line in its place. Should you have any trouble doing this, ask someone at the fly-shop to help you. If you wish, you may add a small piece of wool on the end of the leader to simulate the fly, although to be fair this is not essential.

Fly-rods

Fly-rods are specifically designed for the purpose of fly-fishing and are not that suitable for other forms of angling. Likewise, you cannot effectively fly-cast with an ordinary bait or lure-casting rod; they are designed for different purposes.

The rod in effect allows you, the caster, to load energy into it and release that energy into the line. It is actually perfectly possible to cast without a rod at all, but the rod makes things a whole lot easier and, next to the correct line, is the most critical part of your gear.

Fast and slow actions

Fly-rods are often referred to as having a fast or slow action; this simply means the rate at which they flex and recover to their original shape. Some expensive rods have a form of flex rating on them to distinguish between the faster and slower actions. If you are a novice you need not be overly concerned with this other than to avoid very, very fast-action rods, which will make learning more difficult.

There is a growing, and I believe misguided, trend towards manufacturing rods that have a faster and faster action; that is to say they seem very stiff and flex very rapidly. The idea behind this is that they can cast lines faster and farther, but that is not necessarily true and for the novice it is almost definitely not true. Slower action or 'through action' rods (those that bend throughout as opposed to bending more towards the tip) are far easier to cast, especially for the novice, and the expert caster can cast them just as far as the fast action ones anyway.

Slower action rods also tend to protect delicate tippets (the portion of nylon at the end of the fly-line) from snapping better. This is because a rod that bends throughout can absorb more of the shock that is applied to the line when striking a fish. The same applies to matching rods with a high AFTMA rating to lighter lines. Because the rod does not bend as easily, the line is more likely to snap when pulling on a fish. Many anglers these days find that the latest super-fast and very expensive rod that they have purchased simply isn't as nice to fish with as they thought, and often end up using their old rods because they prefer them.

Particularly if you are a novice, do not be persuaded to get the fastest action rod available as it will make things more difficult for you, especially in the beginning. If you are purchasing tackle for the very first time, once again I urge you to seek out specialist advice at a dedicated tackle store run by fly-fishermen; it will save you a lot of trouble and expense in the long run. Fly-fishing gear is, to a point, like everything else in life; you tend to get what you pay for. At the same time, however, more money may not necessarily equate to better casting performance, especially for the beginner. There are many good rods about

that won't require you to take out a second mortgage to purchase them, but the following points should be borne in mind.

There are very few (if any) good rods that use any material for the handle other than cork rings. If you are offered a foam-handled rod view it with scepticism. Most quality rods suitable for beginners should be made out of carbon fibre, which is remarkably strong and light and has a small diameter, even just above the handle. Unless there are some very specific reasons for it, avoid glass fibre rods with thick diameters. For the most part (and there are exceptions) these rods are cheap and nasty and will hinder your becoming a great caster, which is after all the goal of this book.

The reel

Although fly-anglers like to fuss about this stuff, the reel for the purposes of our exercises is of little importance. When it comes to proper fishing it isn't a whole lot more important, with the exception that it should be as light as possible, and where you are likely to encounter large, fast-swimming fish (saltwater fishing, for example) it should be smooth-running and sturdy too. For now, a reel with enough capacity to hold a hundred metres of backing and the line will serve perfectly well. Once you can impress everyone with your casting, then you can splash out on something expensive so that you look good in all the photographs with your hauls of fish.

The backing

Backing on a fly-reel won't affect your casting at all but it should be mentioned because it is an integral part of your gear. A fly-line is rarely more than 30 metres long (with the price of the stuff you wouldn't want to be paying for line you are unlikely to see), so the reel needs to be 'filled up'. Filling the reel with backing (it's called that because it is at the back of the fly-line) serves two important functions.

Firstly, it prevents the line from being wound too tightly onto the spool, which can result in what is called 'line memory'. Line memory is simply the tendency of the line to form coils from having been wound around a small spool diameter, and can be overcome by selecting quality line, using sufficient backing and even using a large arbour reel (a reel with a large drum).

Secondly, the backing allows you to stay connected to a large, fast-swimming fish should it manage to get more than 30 metres away from you, something that, without backing, would result in the loss of the fish or perhaps even your new and expensive fly-line.

The amount of backing required is determined by how far you think your target fish species are likely to swim away from you, and the space available on the reel. For trout fishing a hundred metres is ample but in saltwater applications you may require several hundred metres, which is one reason why saltwater fly-reels are much larger in the first place.

One final note about backing: do not be tempted to use any old nylon you may find lying about the house. Nylon stretches under tension and, if it is wound back onto the spool, can do damage to the reel. Suitable non-stretch Dacron backing is available at all decent fly-shops.

For the purposes of learning to cast the reel is of little consequence, and as long as it is not overly heavy it will make no difference.

Understanding AFTMA numbers

The AFTMA system was brought about by the need to match the 'power' of fly-rods with suitably weighted lines so that they worked well together. It is far from an exact science, but a lot better than the system that preceded it (which was pretty much guesswork). All you need to know for now is that AFTMA numbers range from 0 to 15 (at least at the last count). All fly-rods will have written on the butt section something like the following:

- '906/5' or 'AFTMA 5' or 'Five-weight' or 'AFTMA 4/5'.
- These would be read as follows:
- '906/5': 'nine-foot, six-inch rod for a five-weight line'
- 'AFTMA 5': 'rod rated as suitable for a five-weight line'
- 'Five-weight': 'rod suitable for a five-weight line'

- 'AFTMA 4/5': 'rod rated as suitable for a line between four-weight and five-weight'.

It can become a little confusing with the multiple numbers such as 4/5 but really the rod manufacturer is simply being honest. If you are casting a long line with such a rod, you may well feel it works better with a four-weight line; if not you may feel it better with a five-weight line. Seek advice from your local fly-shop and if you are a beginner you are probably safest going for the higher number line if there is any doubt.

The way various manufacturers write the information on their rods can be confusing but all of them contain a reference to the line weight suitable for use with the rod.

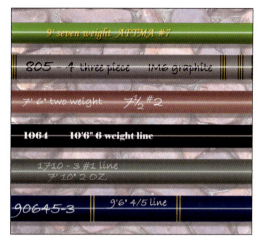

From the top:
A nine foot long rod for a seven-weight line.
An eight foot five inch rod for a four-weight line.
A seven and a half foot rod for a two-weight line.
A ten and a half foot rod for a six-weight line.
A seven foot ten inch rod for a one-weight line.
A nine and a half foot rod for a four- or five-weight line.

These anglers are fishing short and require little casting technique. However, line control and instant response to takes still demand some dexterity.

Success comes to Geoff Ward after making accurate casts under the bushes on the Holsloot River. Many anglers miss out on opportunities such as this, lacking the casting skills and precise presentation required.

What makes a good cast anyway?

How fly-casting really works

Before you start to do the exercises it is important that you understand something of what makes fly-casting work in the first place. I confess I am not sure that anyone really understands how fly-casting works from a scientific point of view. There are a lot of complicated mechanical elements working simultaneously but the equations to explain them in terms of energy transfer, friction, mass and acceleration are not really of too much interest to us.

Thus the explanations in this book are in simple terms. They may, in some cases, not be entirely accurate from a scientific perspective, but they should suffice for you to understand what is going on and what is required of you as the caster. Our goal is not to gain a degree in physics, just to be able to throw an insignificant twist of fur and feather far enough and accurately enough to catch a fish or two.

The importance of the 'loop'

When fly-casting, the fly-line unfurls in the air in the form of a 'loop', unrolling in much the same way as the tracks of a tank would roll. The result is something like that shown in the picture below.

The loop is the most important element of a good fly-cast; in fact you will soon find out that it is virtually the *only* really important element. The better the loop, the better the cast, the

The shape of the line in the air – the 'loop' – is the most critical part of what makes a cast work.

farther it will go, the more accurate the cast will be, the more control you will have and the less effort that will be required. It cannot be overstated that having control over the loop formed when casting is the only really crucial bit of the entire process. Most of the exercises in this book are geared simply to learning how to cast good, tight loops.

A good fly-caster is not one who has miles of line whistling all over the place, or who repeatedly 'shadow casts' with line swirling like a dervish about his head. A good fly-caster consistently throws neat, tight loops of line and you can spot a good caster from a mile away simply by looking at the loops of line he produces when casting.

There is nothing, absolutely nothing, as important as being able to produce neat, tight, stylish loops. Focus your efforts on it and the rewards will be beyond your wildest expectations. Sometimes I think people expect it all to be a lot more complicated than this, but casting good, narrow loops is pretty much all that is needed to gain the results that you want.

Essential casting

Each casting stroke consists of both a back cast (throwing the line behind you) and a forward cast (throwing the line in front of you). If you are casting perfectly these two strokes will be roughly mirror images of one another. Within each cast (backwards or forwards) there are three phases that blend into one another: the tow-in phase, the power snap, and the follow through. This is a lot more difficult to explain than it is to achieve so don't panic.

In this admittedly simplified picture, the angler on the left has produced a formless and open loop which is not good at all, the middle one has better form but is still too wide, whilst the angler on the far right has produced the best loop: tight, even and running parallel to the ground.

Phase 1:
Get the line moving – the tow-in phase

This phase can be ridiculously slow, but its purpose is to start to create some momentum such that the line is not shocked from a standing start, which would cause it to 'bounce'. The tow-in phase both gives the line momentum and removes any slack from the system in preparation for the power snap. Gordon would always describe this phase in terms of towing a car; you ease into it, you don't just let the clutch out and power away.

For the sake of a description we will refer to this as the 'tow-in phase' of the cast. It may seem like you are achieving very little but this phase is an essential step to creating a good cast. Moreover, it needs to be repeated at the beginning of each stroke, whether from a standing start, pulling the line off the water or changing from the forward to the back cast and vice versa.

Phase 1: The tow-in phase, shown here as part of a horizontal cast, is depicted by the light segment in the picture. The tow-in phase is a crucial foundation, getting the line moving and taking any slack out of the system prior to the power snap. (The cast is shown horizontally for better definition.)

Phase 2:
The power snap

This is where it all happens; the rod and line are accelerated in a very short and very quick snap. The power snap creates energy in the rod, which then releases it into the line, accelerating it and creating the line speed and loop required for a good cast.

Despite its name, the power snap doesn't actually require much power, just a severe and short-lived acceleration followed by a rapid deceleration as one enters the follow through. As will be seen later, it is essential that this phase is both brisk and short. This phase is the guts of the entire cast; get it right and the line will sing out in style, get it wrong and you are not going to impress anyone (and your fly won't reach too many fish either).

Phase 2: The power snap (shown as a light colour arc in the image) is the essential element of a good cast; this short, sharp acceleration creates the all-important loop and transfers energy to the line.

Phase 3:
The follow through

This is also an essential element of good casting. Although it doesn't seem to be doing anything at all, it is actually putting the rod in the correct position to be able to start the tow-in phase again. You neglect the follow through at your peril; each casting stroke must contain all three phases.

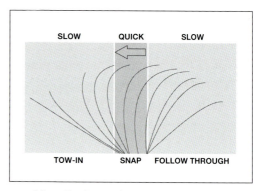

...and then the forward cast

Phase 3: The follow through (shown as a light colour arc in the image) has no effect on the line but is critical in setting up the correct position for the next casting stroke.

In the preceding illustrations notice that the rod tip **IS NOT MOVING IN AN ARC** during the power stroke. It moves in a straight line, and *it is this straight movement that creates the ideal tight loop* and high line speed required to produce a good cast. The ability to produce this flat, straight-line acceleration of the rod tip is at the core of being able to cast well.

So a back cast and forward cast sequence might be illustrated thus: First the back cast...

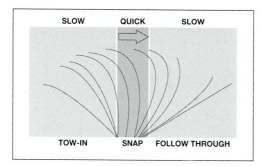

Summary

Each casting stroke consists of three phases:
- Firstly, there is a slow pickup or 'tow-in' phase to get things moving (this occurs when you start a cast and each time you change direction from forward to back cast and vice versa)
- Following the pickup or 'tow-in' phase is a very rapid and short acceleration of the rod tip in a straight line – the 'power snap'
- Finally, you decelerate and follow through in preparation for the next stroke

Remember, to produce a tight loop and an effective cast *the rod tip must move in a straight line* during the power stroke. In order to keep the power stroke going in a straight line it must necessarily be short. Long, sweeping power strokes will always end up moving the rod in an arc, simply because your arms are not long enough to keep up the straight movement.

A little more technical:

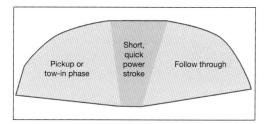

The above diagram shows the movement of the rod tip during a single back cast; note the flat top to the diagram during the power snap.

The image above represents roughly the movement of the rod tip during a single back cast stroke. Note that the effective height or length of the rod diminishes as it bends under pressure; this helps to create the flat trajectory of the power stroke. However, also note that the 'fulcrum' (your hand) of the rod butt is not stationary; the rod butt moves to and fro during the casting stroke. Were it to remain stationary the rod would move in an arc and produce a wide loop, which is worse than useless.

Much existing casting instruction refers to the 'casting clock', which suggests that the rod moves in an arc between 11 and 1 on the clock face. It should be clear from the preceding images that this is absolutely not the case, and we will be dealing more with the casting clock in the section on debunking fly-fishing myths. For now, simply take careful note that the rod does *not* move in an arc during the power stroke of the cast; this is absolutely critical to your ultimate success.

Now you have a basic understanding of the goal in terms of the movement of the rod. Before we get into the exercises though, it is worth taking a few moments to look at what happens in terms of your muscles, nerves and brain when you learn to do something new. It will help you maximise the benefit of the exercises if you understand a little about what is going on in your body whilst you practise. So, on to the learning process...

The learning process

'Creating good habits and teaching your brain to walk and chew gum at the same time.'

To get the best out of this book, and possibly the best out of any other learning process for that matter, it may well help to understand what happens when you set about learning something new. Whether you are driving a car, hitting a golf ball, or touch-typing, the process is much the same, and understanding it may well help you to keep motivated and prevent mistakes in the process. Learning new things can be frustrating at times, but understanding the process should help a lot to keep you on track.

The necessary steps of learning anything

Unconscious incompetence (ignorance is bliss)

What is referred to among scientific boffins as 'unconscious incompetence' basically means that you don't know what you are trying to do and you can't do it (hardly surprising but scientists love these big words). Anyone who has learned to do anything has been at this stage. At some point, you were clueless and the whole process looked completely alien to you. This is actually the best place to start. As you will see later, people with preconceived ideas usually take longer to learn something new, so if you don't have a clue at the moment, you are in the very best position to learn new skills quickly.

Conscious incompetence (the frustration phase)

This is pretty much the next step; you know what you are supposed to do but you still can't. So, for instance, I may know that for me to juggle three balls in the air I must have one in the air all the time, but it doesn't mean that I am capable of doing so. Don't worry about it; you have to know how you are supposed to do something before you can learn to do it. So the first step in any learning process is knowing what you are supposed to do and then practising it. We have already seen that what you need to do to cast well is to move the rod in a manner that will produce a short, sharp power stroke in the middle of the cast. It is just a case of practising the correct form until your brain 'gets it' and your muscles respond automatically to its commands.

Conscious competence (everything is fine so long as you are paying attention)

After some time of practising you will find that you can do what you are supposed to, albeit only when you are concentrating on it. This means that you are now capable of doing a certain task but your body and brain are not yet sufficiently accustomed to it that you can think about something else at the same time. Remember when you used to have to look down at the gearshift of your car when changing from third to fourth?

You don't do that any more because your brain, having repeated the process so many times, now simply shortcuts the complex series of nerve signals and muscle movements into a single packaged response, rather like the shortcut keys on your computer. Press 'Cast' and it all happens as if by magic.

Now there is room for a warning here. Your brain doesn't yet know what is correct and what isn't when it comes to fly-casting, so if you keep practising the wrong thing your brain will produce a shortcut to doing the wrong thing. This is a case of 'garbage in; garbage out'. If you have been fly-casting poorly for some time, this is a potential hiccup for you, because not only do you have to create new shortcuts, you also have to overcome and wipe from your memory the old, bad ones.

To continue the motoring metaphor, have you ever driven someone else's car and kept putting on the windscreen wipers instead of the indicators? That is because your brain has hotwired the 'indicator on' command, but it only works on your car. Be careful what and how you practise. DO NOT PRACTISE ANY OF THE EXERCISES INCORRECTLY, EVER! If you do, you will train your brain and muscles incorrectly and you will then have to reprogramme them all over again.

Practice is the process of creating a habit, albeit a good one, and simple repetition is all that it takes. However, the key issue is to do things correctly. If you are tired, bored or if your mind is wandering, stop. Practise each exercise correctly and carefully every time; it is easy to create good habits but just as simple to create bad ones if you are not diligent.

Unconscious competence (casting and fishing at the same time)

'Unconscious competence' is yet another somewhat highfalutin term for being able to do one thing and chew gum at the same time. You have now mentally ingrained a certain 'packet' of learned behaviour and no longer have to think much about it. If you can change gears in your car whilst looking at the road (a fairly important skill if you are driving), then you are capable of unconscious competence.

Once you have achieved this 'Holy Grail' in terms of fly-casting, you will be able to get on with the serious business of catching fish without spending all of your mental energy on the casting (and without hooking yourself in the ear to boot). It might seem a little way off as you read this, but it is a wholly achievable goal, and achievable in short order if you do things correctly from the start.

Eating an elephant

The old saying: 'How do you eat an elephant? Cut it into bite-sized pieces,' applies here. The exercises in this book are designed to cut fly-casting into bite-sized pieces so that you can ingrain certain movements one at a time without overloading your brain with too much all at once. For this reason the exercises don't always look like fly-casting, but don't worry about it. Each piece will fit together with the next to produce the result you want in the end, I promise. The idea is to 'hot wire' your brain with one movement at a time. You will probably find that some of the exercises take no time at all for your brain to grasp and progress will be both steady and remarkably rapid.

Don't skip

This is a holistic process and you shouldn't skip bits of the learning curve. It is not uncommon for some people to master a particular exercise within minutes, they are not that hard, but it is important that you do go through each one and only move on when you are happy with the results of that exercise. Also, don't be afraid to back up a step or two when things go wrong, as they do for everyone. The exercises allow for a simple means of reaffirming certain aspects when you need to. I have never taught anyone who didn't go back and repeat some of the sections; this is part of your body's learning process.

Forget what you already know

This is a hard one and it isn't (exclusively) the writer being egotistical, but if you fall back into using information that someone else showed you, or that you gleaned from a book or video, then you are very likely to start practising the wrong things again and your casting is not going to improve. To illustrate the point: my ideal pupil would be a female who has never cast a fly-rod in her life. Apart from the obvious allure of teaching women to cast, the fact is that they lack certain traits that most of us men, bless us, just can't seem to escape.

Men seem to have learned that if something doesn't work, we simply try the same thing with more force. Women don't generally do that and therefore focus on the technique more than the power required (fly-casting requires very little power or strength).

Furthermore, someone with no preconceived ideas about what fly-casting is supposed to be like should simply follow the instructions, do the exercises and learn quickly. So, try very hard to ignore anything your fishing buddy, your Alaskan guide or your favourite fishing book says about fly-casting. If you do the exercises detailed in this book it will all come right, REALLY. I have taught some people to cast 15 metres or more in a few minutes and, although it may take some people longer than others, the goal is easily achievable in pretty short order.

Debunking some myths

 Myth 1

The 'casting clock'

This is one time when, if you are a complete novice, you can thank your lucky stars. This is because most people who are reading this will probably already have had some 'tuition' from somewhere, and chances are if they are ever going to become great fly-casters they are going to have to unlearn some of the things they have been taught.

I am sure there are many ways in which to teach someone to cast a fly-rod. However, it is worth mentioning that there are a lot of methods I have seen that, to be honest, really are not that effective (and some which are downright misleading). Forgive me if some of the following upsets a few casting instructors, but the goal of this book is to make you a better caster, in fact to make you a great caster, and if it upsets a few people along the way then it is a small price to pay.

DIRE WARNING: Beware of the 'clock' system of casting instruction. Probably all fly-casters have been shown this method of teaching at some point, and when you consider that an estimated 80% of them still perform poorly it should be enough to convince you that the system doesn't work.

Hundreds of books, magazine articles, fly-casting videos and instruction manuals refer to the casting clock. The idea that the rod moves like the hands of a clock and that the ideal casting stroke occurs between 11 o'clock and 1 o'clock, or something similar, has become something of an angling urban legend and, to be frank, is patently untrue.

I believe that this is the singularly most misleading means of describing how fly-casting works and it is responsible for thousands of frustrated anglers out there casting poorly and not understanding why. The fact that very many instructors use this system is all the more misleading, but I can assure you that I have *never* seen a good fly-caster who actually casts in the manner described by the casting clock system, *not one*. So before you start, if you have experienced this system of tuition in the past, wipe it from your memory. Trust me, it doesn't work, and I am going to take a few moments to describe why it doesn't.

It may seem odd to dedicate a piece of this book so early on to describing what not to do, but the problem is that for many people the idea of the casting clock is almost inextricably ingrained into their fly-casting technique. This system doesn't work, it certainly doesn't

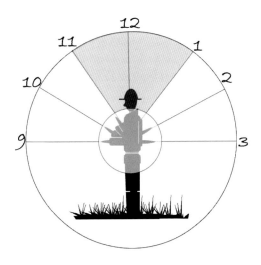

The casting clock suggests that the rod moves in an arc, as do the hands of a clock. This is erroneous and has led to a great deal of confusion for newcomers to fly-casting.

describe accurately what should happen when you are casting, and it has caused huge amounts of confusion for novice fly-casters.

The above illustration is typical of the 'clock casting' system, and it implies that the rod should pivot from the angler's wrist and describe an arc between the times of 11 o'clock and 1 o'clock. Usually it is accompanied by lots of dire warnings that the rod must not go past 1 o'clock. All I can tell you is that this is absolutely untrue. All of the very best casters I have ever watched move the rod through a much wider range and certainly let the rod drift far past the 1 o'clock position. Extending the follow through helps in setting up for the next tow-in phase and doesn't affect the loop. It is only the power stroke that controls the loop.

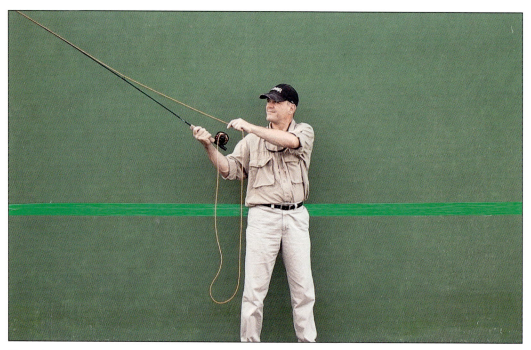

Not only can you extend the rod well past the 1 o'clock position but almost all good casters do so; this follow through is a critical foundation for the next phase of the cast.

 Myth 2

You can measure the effectiveness of your casting by the distance achieved

Measuring your casting competence by the distance you can cast is like measuring your driving skill by how fast you can drive. Good casting is about control, good loop formation and accuracy. Mastering these skills will afford you the ability to cast as far as you want without stress.

So it is important to remember when practising: focus on form, not on distance. Casting long distances comes from good form, not the other way around.

 Myth 3

It is easier to cast with heavier rods and lines

It often seems as though using heavier weight lines makes casting easier, as heavier lines have more mass and more momentum. For this reason, they tend to hide one's mistakes, so on one level your casting may look better and even work a little better to start with. In the end, though, you can learn to cast well with any weight rod and line, and possibly become even more skilful if you use lighter gear.

Fly-rods and their matching lines are designed for different conditions and applications.

No outfit is suitable for every application but good casting will transfer naturally from one set of equipment to another. Learn with whatever you have; it won't actually make any difference in the long run. You can do the exercises in this book with any weight gear from zero to fifteen weight.

Myth 4

You should overload rods with lines heavier than the label says

There are a lot of fly-anglers, fly-shops and instructors who believe this to be beneficial, and in fact it may well be. Overloading a rod will make it behave differently, effectively slowing it down, which many beginners find advantageous. In my opinion many modern fly-rods are underrated in terms of the line that should be used with them. Despite this, however, without a very good reason and sound advice from an expert, you should trust the rod manufacturer to get it right and use the line that is recommended by the AFTMA label. I currently don't overload any of my fly-rods and have yet to feel the need to do so.

Myth 5

To cast well you need power

Perhaps one of the most remarkable things about learning to cast properly is that you will find power is not an issue at all. In fact, many anglers fail because they try to apply too much power. What good casting comes down to is

almost all timing and form. Apart from anything else, using too much power unnecessarily will simply make you tired, and if you get tired you will struggle to cast correctly, and more importantly you will not enjoy your fishing either. So, don't head off to the gym and start lifting weights, you really don't need to.

As I mentioned before, I have often found that many women pick up the fly-casting technique much more quickly than their male counterparts simply because they don't have an automatic response to apply more force when things don't work.

Myth 6

The fault of 'breaking one's wrist'

'Breaking the wrist' is often regarded as a fault in fly-casting, and refers to tipping one's wrist backwards and extending the angle of the wrist and forearm during the casting stroke. Breaking the wrist is not in itself a serious fault, it is the fact that it leads to the movement of the rod in an arc during the power snap that is the real problem.

I have found that the only reason such an action is common is because people tend to stand directly facing their target. This stance puts the shoulder in the way of the rod, restricting the movement of one's arm. Much of the time breaking the wrist can be prevented simply by adjusting the caster's body position to the right or left in such a manner that the casting shoulder is no longer in the way.

Many neophytic casters get all hung up on the problem, but simply focusing on the correct

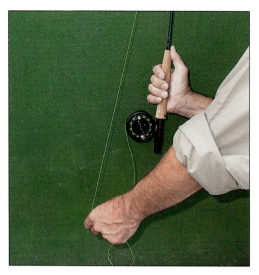

This illustrates 'breaking the wrist': the extension of the angle between the wrist and forearm during the power stroke, which leads to the rod tip moving in an arc, resulting in a poor cast. However, this is usually solved by changing one's stance, and the position of the wrist in the rest of the cast is of little importance.

movement of the rod and keeping the casting shoulder out of the way normally prevents trouble with this supposed 'fault'. Outside of the power stroke you can bend your wrist any way you like without making the slightest bit of difference to your casting stroke.

 ## Myth 7

Fast-action rods cast better

This little story has gained huge popularity of late and manufacturers are continually making faster-action rods to meet market demands. The truth is that if you really are a good caster then a faster-action rod will probably help you cast a bit farther, but at the same time if you are an average caster the chances are that it will make things far worse. It is also much more difficult to 'feel' the line and learn to cast with a fast-action rod.

Also bear in mind that, although this book is about casting, fishing rods are for fishing with, not just casting, and there are a lot of good reasons when fishing to have a rod that is not actually that fast in action. They tend to be less tiring to use, the flexing action makes them easier to become accustomed to, and they protect fine nylon tippets better from breakage when playing fish. Beginners in particular will find it a lot easier to use a rod that is not overly quick to respond.

 ## Myth 8

Distance casting and 'normal' casting are in some way different

I am often asked if I would teach someone 'distance casting', which implies that this is different to teaching people simply to cast well. Truth be told, casting a #2 weight light-trout rod and a #10 weight saltwater outfit rely on exactly the same mechanics. Certainly one can add a few tricks to make distance more achievable, but only as additions to a fundamentally sound casting stroke.

Refer to the sections on **Hauling** and **Double hauling** (pages 70-81), but only after you have mastered the basic cast – even hauling is a technique of far more use than simply to gain more distance.

Myth 9

Wind knots are caused by the wind

'Wind knots' are those nasty little overhand knots that can form in your leader or, in extreme circumstances, in your line while casting. Not only do they reduce the breaking strain of your leader so badly that you would be lucky to land a minnow without the line snapping, they are also a sure indication of poor casting technique, usually where this is combined with the desire to add more power (see **Myth #5** on power).

The concept of wind knots is really just a super way of absolving oneself of responsibility for the result of a poor casting stroke. Wind knots occur most often, though not always, when an angler attempts to overcome the wind by adding more power and changing his or her casting stroke.

You will find more about wind knots later in the section on overcoming common faults. Sorry, but just accept that they are the result of poor form and can be ignored for now. The cure for wind knots is both simple and painless, and we will cover it later in the book.

 ## Myth 10

Good casting is about keeping lots of line in the air and making multiple false casts

It is easy to be impressed with the guy standing on the side of the lake, miles of line swishing and swirling around his head, grunting as he blasts the line into the distance. Very impressive – except that all this is mostly wasted effort.

Good casters NEVER make more than three false casts; that is all that is needed to reach any reasonable target. You will also find that good casting doesn't require much grunting and groaning and, more to the point, very few people catch fish with the line in the air. You want it on the water, where the fish are.

Throughout the exercises in this book, and especially in the later ones where you are making 'proper' overhead casts, don't get into the habit of making too many false casts. One never needs to put all the line in the air to reach a specific distance and line is always let out (shot) at the end of the cast. On short casts you may not be able to shoot out as much line as on long ones but in general *the amount of*

'Wind knots' are not caused by the wind at all but by casting 'tailing loops' where the line crosses itself in the air. A bad fault but one that is easily remedied, there are specific instructions for avoiding this problem later in the book.

line in the air is significantly less than the amount required to reach the desired target.

On shorter casts you may need to aerialise (fly-fishing speak for getting the line into the air with false casts) enough line to cover two thirds of the distance that you actually intend to cover. On long casts, though, expert casters will not aerialise more than about one third of the line needed.

It is entirely possible to cast all 30 metres of a standard fly-line with only one false cast, so don't get caught up in the casting; it might be fun but the point of fishing at the end of the day is catching fish. Also take note that although a lot of fishing videos show a great deal of false casting, this seems to be more for aesthetic value than anything else.

Myth 11

Fly-casting is an 'art'

Fly-casting done well is certainly impressive to watch, but let's call a spade a spade here; it is hardly rocket science. The myth that fly-casting is something beyond mere mortals seems to be holding a lot of people back from learning it. Don't let it hold you back. Anyone can learn to cast fly-fishing gear and I have personally fished with great casters who only had one arm or one hand, so don't go thinking that it is all beyond you.

Once you have learned the lessons in this book by all means you can tell your friends: 'Oh well, of course it's an art', but do be kind enough to point out that it is an art that they too can easily learn.

Myth 12

You can cast to a constant, steady rhythm

The movie *A River Runs Through It* is mostly responsible for this myth, but you absolutely cannot learn to cast by counting out a rhythm to get the timing right. As you have more line in the air, so the tempo slows down; in fact you should think of your rod and line as your metronome. Good casting requires constant adjustment of the stroke tempo as the amount of line in the air varies, from a very quick cycle when casting short, to a much longer cycle when casting a lot of line. With practice your brain will be able to recognise this tempo. Don't try to count or time yourself; simply feel for it as you cast.

Myth 13

Double-taper lines don't cast as well as weight-forward lines

Whilst it is true that weight-forward lines shoot line more effectively by reducing friction, they don't actually cast 'better'. When learning to cast it won't make a jot of difference if your line is weight forward or double taper.

Furthermore, unless you are fishing in a situation where distance is a big issue – on a large reservoir or casting into the surf for example – double taper lines will do a great job. Not only do they present the fly well, but they also have the economic advantage that you can turn them around and use the other end when one end becomes worn or damaged, effectively giving you two lines for the price of one.

Teaching method, grip and stance

We learned early on in the development of this programme that what makes it work is that you only have to learn one thing at a time.

One of the main problems of most fly-casting tuition methods is that you are required to deal with too many things at once. The methodology of this book is to add only one new step to learn at a time; it actually makes one's progress much quicker and more measurable and it also helps one to spot errors quickly before they become ingrained bad habits.

Because of this some of the exercises may not look much like real fly-casting to start with. Don't worry about it, these exercises will result in super casting style in very little time. The system may also seem repetitive on occasion; again this is to be expected, as repetition of each movement until it becomes natural is what will get you casting well in the shortest possible time.

There are a couple of important points about these exercises to note before we begin:

Practising on land, not on water

All of the exercises in this book are designed to take place on grass, not on water. Firstly, water moves, which makes the line more difficult to see and retrieve. Secondly, if you are any kind of aspiring angler then pretty soon you are going to start wondering if there are any fish in the water, and thus lose your concentration on getting the casting right. So, find a nice piece of level grass that has been cut short and get down to business.

This is the basic stance for almost all of the exercises in the book. Note the horizontal rod position, the hand turned so that the reel is parallel with the ground and the slight angle of the body to the direction of the cast.

The exercises are not actual casting to start with

Although most actual fly-fishing in real life takes place with the rod in an almost vertical plane, most of the exercises in this book operate on a horizontal one. The reason for this is that it allows you to see the line in the air much more easily and to stop in the middle of a cast whenever you wish. Don't let this concern you, as the action is near identical. Later on the plane will be changed to the vertical, but for most of the exercises this will be the basic position.

Basic position

In learning to fly-cast there are only a couple of things about your body that are really important. You will notice that there is little mention of what to do with your wrist, your elbow or your left knee; it really doesn't matter that much and through the exercises your body will work all of that out for itself quite happily. What does really matter is how you hold the rod and how you position your body. The correct grip and stance are essential to learn, let alone master, good casting.

The horizontal grip transforms to this position when you start casting on a vertical plane later in the exercises, but note that the thumb is still opposite the reel.

The grip

Again there are some who would dispute this (as the adverts say: 'There's always one, isn't there!'), but trust me when I tell you that you want to have the thumb of your casting hand opposite the reel. That means in normal vertical casting the thumb will be pushing the forward cast, and in our method, for most of the exercises, it will be horizontal and opposite the reel.

What should be obvious from the pictures is that the grips are the same; you are just holding the rod in different planes, and that is what you want. But why should you hold the rod like this?

The continental grip as shown doesn't result in better casting accuracy and is unsuitable for use with heavy tackle.

Why is the grip that important?

The reasons are simple: your thumb moves more easily in a straight line than your forefinger and it is a whole lot stronger than your forefinger (that's why they're called 'thumb tacks', not 'forefinger tacks'). Grips that use the forefinger in the position shown on the bottom left put excessive strain on your finger joints and are not effective with heavy tackle. Rather start out the way you plan to continue.

Some anglers believe that having the forefinger opposite the reel offers more accuracy, but in our testing this was never the case. In addition, it puts massive strain on your forefinger when casting heavy saltwater gear, so use your thumb. After all, only higher primates have opposable thumbs, so you may as well use your privilege to good effect.

Gripping the rod as one would a racquet doesn't work either, because you lack control and at the same time have to grip the rod harder, leading to tiredness and poor technique.

Some beginners tend to hold the rod as shown. It is not possible to cast well holding the rod like this; without the thumb the rod tends to arc. To prevent this one has to grip it much tighter, resulting in fatigue.

The stance

When casting, position your body as shown in the picture to the right; that is to say off at an angle from the direction of the cast. Stand with your feet just more than shoulder width apart and with your body angled some 35° to the right of the target (for a right-handed caster) or 35° to the left of the target (for a left-handed caster).

Standing perpendicular to the casting direction was at one time considered quite the 'right thing to do', though I frankly have no idea why. Standing in such a manner will cause you no end of trouble as your rod hand will find your shoulder in the way when it comes to make the back cast. This will force you to tip the rod backwards in an arc, something we already know is a pretty hopeless position for casting. Some anglers do still seem to manage to cast like this but I assure you that they achieve results *despite* this position and not *because* of it.

I have solved numerous anglers' casting problems by doing little more than grabbing them and turning them a little to get their shoulder out of the way. So, position your body with your legs a little more than shoulder width apart and facing about 35° to the side of the target.

In an actual fishing situation it may not always be possible to get into this ideal position. However, you will usually find that you can get close enough, and you will rarely find that you have to stand directly facing your target, even in the most overgrown streams. Remember that the best stance is one that gets your shoulder out of the way and allows your arm to move freely.

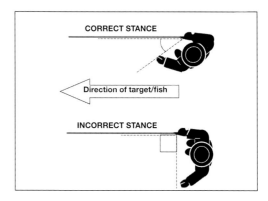

This picture demonstrates the difference between the correct and incorrect stance for a right-handed caster practising horizontal exercises. The same stance is used when making overhead casts later, the rod is simply lifted to a vertical position.

Holding the line

Later on your non-casting hand is going to be responsible for line control, but for the first few exercises simply tuck the line under the fingers of your casting hand, hold it firmly against the rod handle so that it doesn't slip, and do the exercises with the same amount of line out all the time.

That's it; once you have the correct grip and stance do whatever feels natural to you in the exercises. As I said, your body will sort the rest out for itself over time. Your body has been around with you since you were born and it is quite good at working out what it is that you want it to do if you give it a chance. One final point, if you are left-handed you will notice that most of the images and diagrams show a right-handed caster. Simply position yourself in a mirror image of the pictures, or look at the images in a mirror until you get the hang of things.

Start off with the line simply trapped under the forefinger of the casting hand as shown; however, for the exercises twist the rod so that the reel is parallel to the ground.

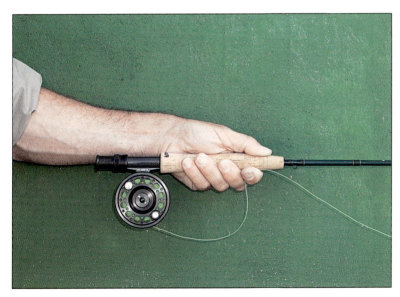

The grip for the left-handed caster is simply a mirror image.

Main picture: *One last fish to the author as a wonderful day's fishing comes to an end in the Richtersveld.*
Top: *Deep wading shouldn't upset your casting.*
Middle: *Anglers fishing a 'hot spot' on the Orange River.*
Bottom: *Dale Stephenson with a bright silver largemouth yellowfish from the Orange River.*

Getting the feel of it

This is a brief but particularly important exercise for the complete novice, though even those with some experience of casting fly-fishing gear should consult it as it serves to reinforce the essential style of this teaching method. As mentioned previously, the real benefit of this method is that it allows you to add one step at a time and therefore master one element per exercise. The horizontal casting stroke is the basis for all the steps to follow.

For the novice, the purpose of the exercise is simply to get used to the feel of the gear. If you have previously used only other kinds of tackle, the entire outfit is likely to feel somewhat strange. The rods used in fly-fishing are very light and soft in action compared to other types of tackle so it is just a case of getting a feel for things. It shouldn't take more than about 15 minutes.

Tackling up for the first time

First of all, thread the fly-line through each of the guides on the rod. The tiny ring just above the handle on some rods is to hold the fly when walking about; do not thread the line through this one! Pull approximately 7 metres or so of fly-line out of the top of the rod and hold the line coming off the reel against the handle grip with the forefinger of the rod hand.

Next, stand in the position shown in the previous pictures, with feet slightly wider apart than your shoulders and your body at approximately 35° off line to the direction of your casts. This will take your casting shoulder out of the way and 'free up your arms' for a clean casting stroke. Hold the rod parallel with the ground at the same height as your hip with your hand tilted upwards so that the reel is also

---

Requirements

- A level grass area, for instance a lawn or rugby field, with enough space to cast the line 10 metres or so in front of and behind you
- A fly-rod and reel with a floating line, preferably of a highly visible colour, and of the same AFTMA rating as the rod
- A level 'leader' of monofilament nylon tied to the front of the line

For the horizontal practice exercises hold the rod as shown, though to start with trap the line under the forefinger of your casting hand. Note the reel is parallel to the ground and the thumb is opposite the reel.

parallel to the ground. This may seem a little unnatural at first, but when we later convert the stroke to the vertical plane it will be obvious that this is in fact the correct orientation.

Simply flip the line in front of you parallel with the ground and let it land, then flip it back the other way and let it land again. You should repeat this process, one step at a time, until you feel comfortable with the grip and the weight of the tackle in your hand. It doesn't matter what the casting stroke looks like, this exercise is just for you to get used to the orientation of the rod; this will be used in the rest of the exercises in this book.

Just focus on keeping the rod parallel to the ground and your wrist orientated in such a manner that the reel is also horizontal to the ground and the thumb of the casting hand is opposite the reel.

In the next exercise we will add some elements to make the cast work more effectively.

Make one cast at a time, backwards first; note the position of the rod and the reel being held parallel to the ground and the line trapped under the forefinger of the casting hand.

Follow each back cast with a forward one after allowing the line to land on the ground. Repeat.

Key elements

- Adopt the correct stance
- Use the correct grip with thumb opposite the reel
- Hold the line tightly against the rod handle with the casting hand
- Only make one cast at a time
- Get a feel for the way the tackle responds
- Get used to the orientation of the tackle for the forthcoming exercises
- Ensure that you stop and let the line land on the ground with each stroke
- Don't worry what the line looks like in the air at this point

Problems to watch out for

- Changing your grip or the orientation of the rod

Changing speeds during the casting stroke

As with all the following exercises, we will now add a single additional element to the previous exercise. Holding the rod in the same manner and with the same grip, line trapped against the reel handle, repeat the process as in Exercise 1.

However, this time you can start working on making a nice, tight loop. This is achieved by changing the speed of the stroke from slow to quick and back to slow again. The quick part of the stroke is called the 'power snap', even though it doesn't really require much power. The key elements are to make the power snap quick and short, with the rod tip moving in a straight line during the snap.

Make a horizontal back cast first. Start the cast with a slow tow-in phase, quickly accelerate and then slow down again in the follow through; don't forget to let the line land on the ground behind you.

It is essential to follow through, as this puts the rod in the correct position for the slow start of the forward cast to follow. Then make a forward cast in the same manner. At this stage make each stroke separate, letting the line land on the grass at the end of each individual stroke.

You should rapidly notice that compared to Exercise 1, you now have some control of the shape and size of the loop formed in the line. The more distinct the power stroke and the straighter the line of the rod tip during the

The back cast is simply that phase of the stroke that sends the line behind you. Accelerate the movement during the power stroke (depicted as a pale section in the picture on the left), keep the movement short and the rod tip moving in a straight line.

Repeat the process with a similar forward cast: slow, quick, slow, and let the line land on the ground. In this composite image you can see the rod in the tow-in phase and the formation of a nice, tight loop at the end of the power snap.

Moving the rod tip in an arc during the power stroke will result in a wide and poorly formed loop and a consequentially poor cast. Note the wide loop being formed in the line.

power stroke, the better the loop. Also note it has very little to do with the amount of force you use; it is counter-productive to try to force the cast. Just slow...snap...follow through on each separate stroke.

Be extremely precise when practising this exercise, as you are trying to ingrain the correct motion. If you do the exercise incorrectly then that is what your brain and muscles will learn to do.

Repeat the forward and backward strokes as many times as you need to until you start getting some consistency. Make each stroke an individual effort; we will link them together later. If you get tired then stop. Practising when you are tired will undo the good that you have done.

By the time you are ready to move to the next exercise you should notice that the line is pulling against your fingers at the end of each stroke as though it wants to keep going all on its own. This is a sure sign that you are making good loops and that the energy transfer from the rod to the line is becoming more effective and efficient.

Only make one stroke at a time and let the line land on the ground after each stroke.

Key elements

- Maintain the same stance, horizontal rod position, correct thumb position and grip on the line as in Exercise 1. Change the speed of the movement in a three-phase stroke
- Snap the power stroke in a short, straight line
- Note that the rod hand moves and doesn't just pivot
- Watch for the change in the loop of line; it will get narrower when you get it right
- Notice the line 'pulling out' at the end of each stroke when you make a narrow loop
- Don't try to force the cast; you don't need to apply a lot of power

Problems to watch out for

- Holding the rod away from your body. 'Reaching' doesn't do much harm but it will make you tired quickly
- Trying too hard. Be aware that you may try to simply force the cast and still swing the rod in an arc. Remember that you don't need power to achieve results
- Changing the grip; you are probably not yet comfortable with the horizontal grip, so take care not to change it
- Having too much line out. Avoid the temptation to have too much line on the ground; at this stage you are only working on form, not on distance

Adding a point of reference

This time, using the same stance, grip and orientation of the rod, we will be working on further improving the loop formed in the line as you cast. To assist in this endeavour we are now going to add a point of reference. On the ground in front of you, position a rod case or any straight object approximately the length thereof (roughly 1 metre). Use this marker to show you the range of the power stroke.

Make the same strokes that you did in Exercise 2 and focus on moving the rod tip in a straight line as you make the power stroke. Remember that it is the power stroke alone that determines what the line does, nothing else.

Again focus on each forward and backward stroke as individual elements. You are further ingraining the required response from your muscles, nerves and brain that will eventually result in automatic execution of perfect casts over and over again.

During this exercise you should really be able to feel the line pulling as though it wishes to carry on going at the end of each cast. This is essential before moving on to the next exercises as this means that you are making better loops and transferring energy from the rod to the line with greater efficiency. These are the essential elements that will help build towards flawless casting.

Using a marker can assist in positioning the power snap at the correct point in the stroke. In this case, a rod tube is being used as a marker. Your fishing line should unroll in a straight line parallel with the marker.

Here the tow-in phase of a back cast is about to be completed and as the rod reaches the marker, the power snap will commence.

Key elements

- Shorten the power stroke and keep it straight
- Reduce the width of the loop even further
- Feel the rod begin to 'load' as it stores energy during the brief power stroke
- Continue to make individual forward and back casts, one at a time
- Be sure to maintain the same stance, thumb orientation and body position as in the previous exercises

Problems to watch out for

- Swinging the tip of the rod too far around during the power stroke and opening the loop
- Dropping the position of the reel and 'hitting a tennis shot'

INCORRECT: Extending the power stroke for too great a distance results in the tip moving in an arc and large, poorly formed loops in the line.

The correct position (above) and the incorrect (below). In the lower image the grip has been rotated so that the rod is held like a tennis racket – take care not to fall into this trap.

Joining the back and forward cast into a complete stroke

Using the same grip, stance, and orientation of the rod as in the previous exercises, we shall once again add another single element. This time we will be joining the back cast and forward cast together into one fluid casting motion, but still we will only make one full cast at a time. Back cast move...snap... follow through...forward cast...move...snap... follow through...let the line land on the grass in front of you. You may wish to keep the point of reference of a line or rod case in place for this exercise to reinforce the position of the power stroke.

This might at first seem far more complicated than the previous exercises but we have only added one new thing. The key is correctly timing when to commence the forward cast.

It is almost inevitable that you will try to start the forward cast too early to begin with, and with too much power and speed. Resist the temptation to rush things. You have plenty of time.

Simply start the forward cast just before the line straightens at the end of the back cast and maintain the same tempo. Don't rush; if it clips the ground a few times it won't matter. This will take a little practice and almost certainly you will need to go back to Exercise 3 a few times to re-establish the basic stroke. Don't worry about it; once you have the basic stroke working properly again, try to join them together into a single fluid movement.

Back cast...move...snap...follow through... forward cast...move...snap...follow through... let the line land on the grass. You are now for the first time making complete casting strokes! Maintain focus on the shape of the loop and the concise, straight snap of the power stroke that will create neat, narrow loops.

The transition from back cast to forward cast starts with the tow-in phase of the latter, just as the line straightens behind you.

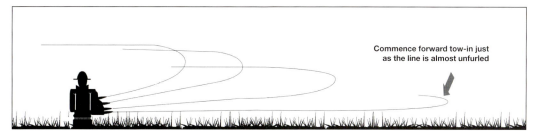

Commence forward tow-in just as the line is almost unfurled

Be sure not to rush the forward cast; give the line time to unfurl.

Key elements

- Keep the same pace and three-speed movement ingrained in previous exercises
- Control the desire to hurry the forward cast; there is plenty of time to make it
- Take particular care not to skip the tow-in phase of the forward cast
- Watch the line to help you get the timing correct. With practice you will no longer need to watch as you will be able to feel the weight of the line telling you to commence the forward stroke
- Make only one casting cycle at a time and land the line in front of you at the end of every complete cast

Problems to watch out for

- Trying to rush and overpower the forward stroke, skipping the tow-in phase. Focus on keeping the same style and tempo as before; this is the most important part of the exercise

Multiple casting strokes

This is just a simple extension of the previous exercise (remember that each little step forward will build into perfect casts in no time at all), but it is necessary to go through each phase until you are comfortable with it. In fly-casting it is often necessary to make more than one complete stroke sequence and so, just as you have practised the transition from back cast to forward cast, you will now add the transition from forward to back cast.

Using the same stance, grip, etc. as before, make a complete stroke, tow-in...snap...follow through...tow-in...snap...follow through as in Exercise 4 but this time continue into another cycle and complete a further back cast and

forward cast before stopping. This demands an additional element: the timing of the commencement of the back cast and, just as before, that is when the line is almost straight out, this time in front of you.

Make two or three complete cycles of forward and back casts and then let the line fall down on the ground again. Just as with the previous exercise you will find that there is a natural tendency to speed up, rush things and miss out the tow-in phase of the cast. Focus on maintaining the same tempo as previously and don't be afraid to go back to Exercise 4 or even 3 if you feel that you need to.

The key elements of this exercise are the transitions between each casting stroke, as shown in this composite image. Remember not to rush the transition from the forward to back cast and vice versa.

Key elements

- Watch to determine the exact timing of the transition from one direction of cast to the next
- Be careful to maintain the three-speed movement throughout each and every casting stroke
- Only make two or three complete transitions at a time and then land the line on the grass
- Concentrate on keeping the rod horizontal throughout

Problems to watch out for

- Trying to speed up and force the cast; keep the same tempo
- Focusing on only the back or forward cast; you should be aiming for good form throughout the entire cycle
- Changing the orientation of the rod. Keep it horizontal; you will start with overhead casts shortly

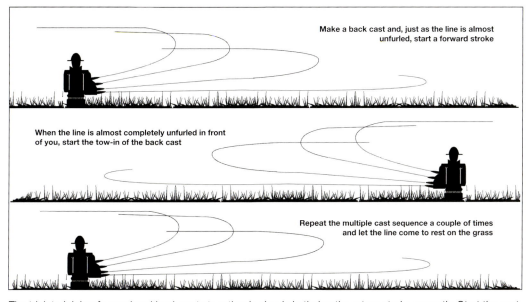

Make a back cast and, just as the line is almost unfurled, start a forward stroke

When the line is almost completely unfurled in front of you, start the tow-in of the back cast

Repeat the multiple cast sequence a couple of times and let the line come to rest on the grass

The trick to joining forward and back casts together is simply in timing the return stroke correctly. Start the next tow-in phase just before the line straightens out. You will have to watch for this to start with but with practice you will be able to tell when the time is right without looking.

Proper overhead casts for the first time

By now you should be able to make multiple casting strokes whilst maintaining a good, neat, tight loop shape in the line on both the forward and back casts. This exercise will start the transition from horizontal exercises to proper overhead casting. Bear in mind, however, that there is really no 'correct' angle to cast at, and in various situations whilst fishing you may find it useful to cast with the rod anything from completely vertical to horizontal. The

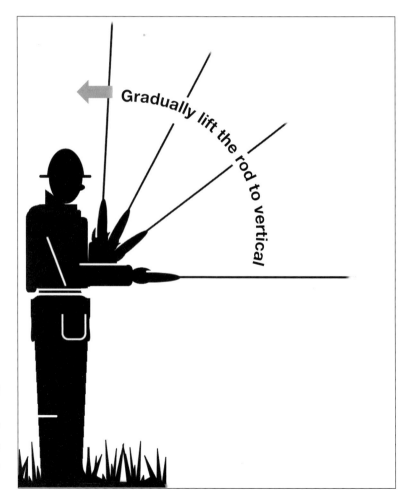

Gradually lift the rod to vertical

Making multiple casts, gradually lift the rod more and more vertical. Keep the orientation of the line, reel and casting hand the same relative to one another.

important thing is that the same stroke is used and the same orientation of the rod, line and hand is maintained.

To start moving towards vertical casting, begin in exactly the same manner as in the previous exercise. Make several linked back and forward casts without stopping. Then continue to do the same thing again, but this time gradually lift the rod upwards at a steadily increasing angle from the horizontal to the vertical plane with each successive casting stroke.

Nothing should change except the angle of the rod, line and hand, all of which should move into a more vertical position together. Be sure to keep the thumb opposite the reel. It is essential that the relationship between hand, rod and line trajectory remains the same relative to each other.

Key elements

- Again only one change is made, the variation of the angle of the cast from horizontal to vertical
- Make the change gradually as you keep the line in the air with multiple casting strokes
- Change the angle of everything at the same time. The thumb moves into a vertical plane with the rod, the line moves into a vertical plane in line with the rod; everything is moved to the new angle at the same time

Problems to watch out for

- Moving the angle of the rod and 'leaving the line behind'. By the time the rod is vertical the line should be moving above the tip of the rod, not underneath or to the side of it
- Turning the body to a perpendicular position relative to the cast; this will cause all manner of problems. If you feel that your shoulder is getting in the way of your stroke you have unconsciously turned or started to cast in a different direction
- Loss of timing in any of the elements of the cast. If this happens go back and repeat some of the previous exercises until you feel comfortable with the results
- Casting the line at the ground or up into the air; the loop should unfold roughly parallel to the ground if you have made the transition to vertical casting correctly

Line control with your non-casting hand

Well done, by now you should be making your first 'proper casts'. You should also be able to see a massive improvement in the speed of the line, the shape of the loop and the ease with which you can make multiple stylish casting strokes.

Now that you have gained the ability to make vertical casts it is time to start using your other hand in the casting process. You cannot actually fish and control the line with one hand; it is impractical, so having made some basic progress with the fundamentals of

Repeat Exercise 5, using your non-casting hand to hold the line tight; this should simply assist you in acclimatising to the use of your other hand in controlling the line.

casting it is time to introduce the non-casting hand into the picture.

Until now you should have been holding the line trapped between the fingers of your casting hand and the rod handle. Now, release the line from your rod hand and hold it in your non-casting hand between thumb and forefinger.

Soon you are going to use this hand to both hold the line tight, and let it slip out of your fingers when you wish to lengthen the cast. For now, however, simply hold it tight.

Go back to exercises 5 and 6, and repeat some multiple casting strokes simply holding the line in your non-casting hand. It isn't difficult and shouldn't take more than a couple of tries to get used to the new position.

Resist the temptation to pull the line with your non-rod hand at this point; we will come to that later. For now, simply hold it tight and repeat Exercise 6. If necessary do some of the other exercises over again with the line held in the non-rod hand to help you get used to it.

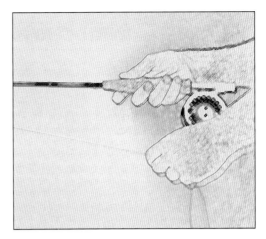

Simply hold the line tight in your non-casting hand instead of against the rod handle as previously.

Key elements

- **The only thing that has changed is that you are now holding the line in your non-rod hand; this shouldn't affect the casting stroke in any way at all**
- **Keep the non-rod hand still during the casting stroke and at about waist level to reduce the amount of slack introduced during the forward cast**
- **There should otherwise be no real trouble with this exercise but make sure you hold the line tight for the present time; you will be letting out more line in the next exercise**

Problems to watch out for

- **Pulling the line with your non-rod hand**

Shooting line: the 'acid test'

This really is the 'acid test', because if you have by now mastered the ability to cast tight loops of line, the whole thing should work just fine. If you are not casting good loops, however, you will know soon enough because the line will not shoot out properly. Think of this exercise as a way of confirming that you have learned the basics well, and if it doesn't work it is simply an indication that you need to go back and practise your casting stroke some more.

Position yourself with about 10 metres of the fly-line on the ground and the rod held horizontal, reel opposite your thumb and also parallel to the ground. Pull about 1 metre of extra line off the reel behind your non-casting hand as shown below.

Make several linked forward and back casts, in exactly the same manner as previously;

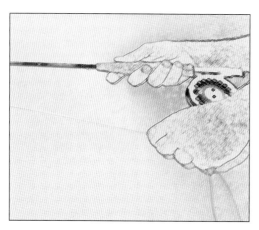

Extra line is held as shown, ready to be shot out at the completion of the final forward cast by simply letting it slide through your fingers.

however, this time when you are feeling comfortable on the forward cast simply let the line slide through your fingers and 'shoot' out of the rod tip, lengthening the cast.

The key elements of this exercise are loop shape and timing. If you have progressed to this point, the loop shape should already be good, and the timing is simply a matter of when to let go of the line with your non-casting hand. If you let go too early (during the power snap), all of the power of the cast will be lost. If you let go too late, then the line will be pulled to a halt and the momentum lost, resulting in the line not shooting out properly. *The correct time is just after the loop has formed, that is a moment or two after the power stroke.* The loop in the line acts just like a weight, and once formed it is going to go wherever you have sent it, taking the extra line with it.

You will need to practise to get the timing of letting the line go just right, but with time it will become instinctive and, like all the other exercises in this book, pretty soon you won't have to think about it at all. Do not be afraid to go back to the previous exercises, even if you leave the line now trapped in your non-casting hand. You have to be able to generate line speed through a tight loop, and the ability to shoot the line will rely largely on whether the loop is narrow enough.

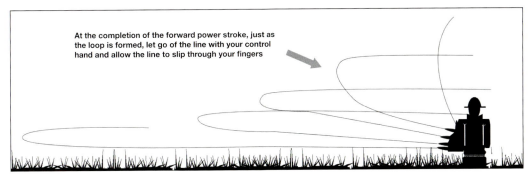

At the completion of the forward power stroke, just as the loop is formed, let go of the line with your control hand and allow the line to slip through your fingers

Release the line just as the loop is formed. The kinetic energy in the loop will pull more line with it, extending the range of the cast.

Key elements

- Make good, tight loops with lots of momentum
- Let the line slip through the fingers of your non-casting hand at the right time, just after the power stroke
- Still maintain the same horizontal form that you have throughout the majority of the exercises

Problems to watch out for

- Letting the line go too soon (during the power stroke): all power is lost and the line won't go anywhere
- Letting the line go too late: the line will 'tug' on your hand and bounce back before it has a chance to go anywhere
- Not forming tight loops: as mentioned, this is the acid test, and if your loops are poor they will not have sufficient momentum to carry the extra line with them. If this is the fault then go back to the previous exercises until the loop is looking tighter and you can feel it pulling against your hand at the end of each stroke

Additional line control and handling

When you are fishing, it is the non-rod hand that is responsible for the majority of line control. There are three primary positions of the hand during casting, fishing or retrieving the line.

The first position is the casting position, where the non-casting hand holds the line tight; this is essential for casting and striking any fish that might take your fly.

The second is the retrieval position, when you are pulling line in to cast again, or retrieving line to stay in contact with the fly, or to move the fly in an enticing manner for the fish. When retrieving line you use the index finger of your casting hand as a 'pulley' so that you can pull line in with your non-casting

hand with control. When pulling line in let the line slide between the index finger of your casting hand and the rod handle. This position also allows you to quickly trap the line under your finger when a fish takes and you need to strike. When you are ready to cast again you release the line from your casting hand.

Thirdly, there is the 'shooting line' position. When shooting the line during a cast, you can simply let the line go, but you have a lot more control if you form an 'O' with the thumb and index finger of your non-casting hand and let the line slide freely through it. This way you can grab the line at any time and start casting again without having to look down, an important skill in fly-fishing.

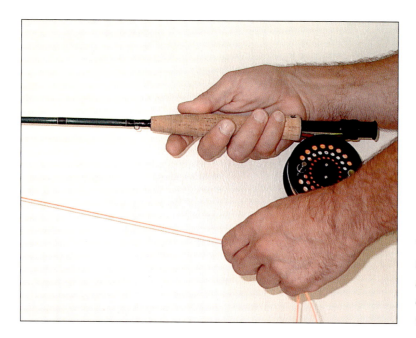

The casting position: Holding the line in the non-casting hand is essential for control when fishing.

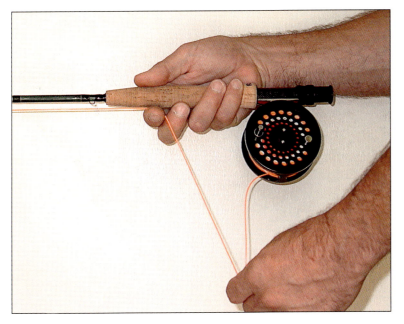

The retrieval position: notice how the forefinger of the casting hand is used as a pulley, so the line can be allowed to slip under the finger or trapped as required.

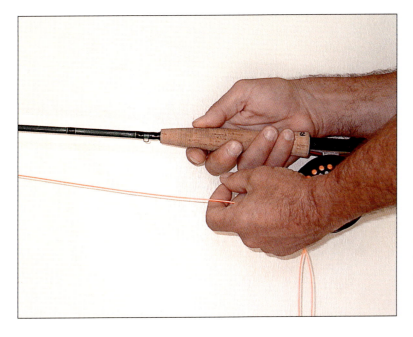

The 'shooting line' position: releasing line through an 'O' formed by your fingers means that you never lose control of the line.

Practise all three different positions

Make horizontal casts with the line held tightly in your non-casting hand. Refer to the image of the casting position (see page 60).

On the final delivery, as with Exercise 8, shoot some line on the forward cast, this time taking care to form an 'O' with the thumb and forefinger of your non-rod hand so that you don't drop the line, and then let the cast land on the ground. Refer to the image of the shooting line position (see page 61).

Without looking down, place the line over the forefinger of your casting hand and, using it as a pulley, pull the extra line that you shot out back in again.

Once you have pulled a metre or so of line back in, release the line from your casting hand and repeat the entire process. Although you are still casting on the horizontal plane, this is very much like what you will be doing when you are actually fishing.

Repeat this exercise until you are comfortable managing the line without looking down at your hands; once you can do this exercise smoothly you are ready to go and actually do some fishing!

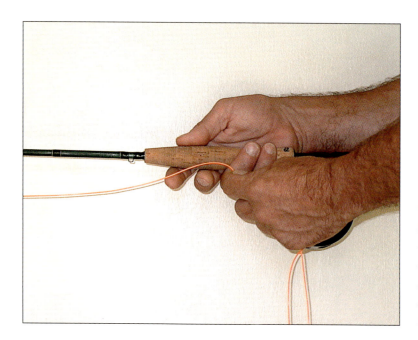

Replacement of the line back onto the 'pulley' of your forefinger after each cast is an essential skill and needs to be accomplished without looking down.

Key elements

- Manage the line correctly with the non-casting hand
- Practise the three line-control positions: casting, shooting and retrieving line
- Aim to be able to perform the sequences without having to look at your hands
- Use the forefinger of the casting hand as a pulley
- Maintain contact with the line all the time and don't drop it

Problems to watch out for

- Looking at your hands. The goal is to be able to do these exercises without looking at your hands, so take care not to get into the habit of looking down. With a bit of practice, you can easily learn to touch your hands together and transfer the line from one position to the other without looking
- Letting go of the line completely. It can be tempting to let go of the line; this will cause you problems when you are actually fishing. You should have control of the line at all times
- Neglecting the basics. Although this exercise is about line control you should still be making neat, clean casting strokes, shooting line and reaffirming all the exercises that you have completed to date. Don't let your form slip back into poor habits just because the focus is on line management

Putting it all together in the vertical plane

This exercise is virtually a repeat of Exercise 6; the only difference is that now you are controlling the line with the non-casting hand. Starting in the horizontal position and casting as in Exercise 9, keep the line in the air, making multiple casting strokes. Do not shoot out any additional line at this point.

Gradually raise the rod into the vertical position, maintaining the same tempo and line control that you have already practised. Once you are making casts in the vertical plane, release the line on the forward cast, allowing it to slip through the fingers of your non-casting hand and land on the ground.

Congratulations, you should now be making proper overhead casts with perfect line control and you are ready to go fishing. You have mastered the basics of quality casting. From here on, the exercises are all about building on these basic skills to enhance your ability further. Don't stop practising now; you should be a good caster at this point, now is the time to turn yourself into a great caster.

Key elements

- Make the change gradually as you keep the line in the air with multiple casting strokes
- Change the angle of everything at the same time

Problems to watch out for

- Managing the line correctly. If you have trouble with the line management go back to Exercise 9
- Not maintaining the correct orientation of hand, rod and line trajectory. If you have trouble moving the cast to the vertical position, review Exercise 6

Correcting various faults

Chances are by now that things are going well, but at the same time you may have problems with some common faults. We haven't focused on faults much up until now because once you understand all the basics of casting it is easy to remedy the most common casting errors. The following are some 'remedial' steps to assist you if you find that you have a pernicious little habit that just won't go away.

Slack line when you commence a casting stroke

When fishing or practising making vertical-plane casts it is essential that you start the first back stroke holding the rod low with the line tight, such that lifting the rod to begin the back cast will start to move the line immediately. If you start the cast with the rod tip held too high, you will have too much slack line hanging from the tip to cast properly. Remember, the line must be taut throughout the duration of the entire casting stroke to make it work properly.

Forced open loops

This can be tricky to spot. It seems as though you are doing it all correctly; the power snap is short and flat, but the loop is still wide and has no real power. This can be caused by not slowing the rod down sufficiently after the power stroke, 'dragging the loop open' after it has been formed. To help overcome this problem I often put something in the way of the caster to prevent an early follow through.

Using the same stance, etc. as used in all the horizontal casting exercises, place a stick or have a person stand in the way as shown in the picture on page 66. By stopping the follow through completely you will find that your power stroke gets sharper.

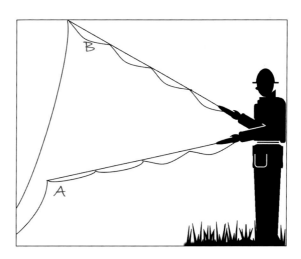

Starting the cast with the rod tip too high, as in position 'B', leaves slack line that has to be picked up before the casting stroke commences. It is better to lower the rod to 'A', pull in any slack line and start the cast from there.

After a while you can remove the obstacle and carry on with a normal follow through. It is very important that there is a distinct pause or slowing down of the stroke just at the end of the power snap to allow the loop to form.

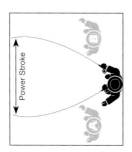

Stand someone in the way to prevent you from following through too much or too early.

Either your forward or back cast is better than the other

This is so common that to start with it is virtually guaranteed. I find when teaching that somewhere in the region of 70% of people find it much easier to make a good cast on forward stroke and the other 30% for some reason find that their back cast is better. Either way, the answer is simply to practise the basic horizontal casting exercises, watching both casts very carefully for signs of a poor loop.

A major fault of most anglers, and in particular beginners, is simply that they view the back cast as less important. After all, the fish are out there in front of you, right? The back cast is of equal importance to the forward cast, as it is the foundation of a good forward cast. Lack of line speed or control of the back cast will lead to slack in the line and nothing to 'pull against' when you make the forward stroke.

Don't be tempted to ignore your back cast and, for goodness' sake, do watch the line so that you can monitor the loop as you cast. If you find this is difficult, simply go back to the basic horizontal casting exercises and focus on whichever direction of cast you feel is problematic.

Hitting the rod with the line

Again, almost everybody does this sometimes, perhaps because of awkward winds, but it shouldn't happen that often. The primary reason for this happening is moving the rod in exactly the same plane on the forward and back casts. Most casters have a slight variation of the plane of the cast from forward to back that avoids this happening, as though the rod tip moves through a very slight ellipse during the stroke. Be careful, however, not to start swinging the rod around your head in a circle.

The other way to avoid this is to cast the line slightly upwards and away from the rod tip as you cast, and to follow through with a deliberate tipping of the rod tip downwards to get it out of the way.

Moving the rod in a slight (emphasis on slight) elliptical motion will help avoid the line hitting the rod. The rod travels on a slightly different path on the forward and backward strokes, but don't overdo it.

Casting 'wind knots'

'Wind knots' are caused by throwing what are known as 'tailing loops', which are bad news but easy to solve. There are a couple of possible reasons why anglers throw tailing loops. Although our discussion focuses on making tailing loops on the forward cast, it is just as easy to make them on the back cast so watch out, all those knots might be forming behind you when you aren't looking.

Problem number one:

The power stroke, or haul when hauling (see later), is brought in too early in the stroke, which is to say before the rod has reached vertical. This is why it seems as though the wind knots are caused by overpowering the cast, such as trying too hard for distance or trying to cast into the wind. It isn't the power that causes the tailing loop, but rather the position of the rod when the power is applied. To remedy this, simply start the power stroke a little bit later than you have been doing; you will find the loop forms perfectly the minute you do this.

Problem number two:

This looks very much the same as the above; however, the power stroke is started with the rod vertical but then the rod tip is tipped backwards again as the caster brings their elbow forward, rather as if playing a squash shot or throwing a cricket ball. It is no coincidence that this particular flaw is very common in cricketers and squash players. Be sure to move the rod in a straight line during the power stroke.

Problem number three:

We have yet to discuss hauling, but as a reference for the future the third most common cause of tailing loops is putting the haul into the cast at the incorrect point. Hauling is merely a way of adding additional line speed during the power snap of the cast, so if you put the haul in with the rod tipped backwards (on the forward cast) you will again cause a tailing loop.

Wind knots are caused by tailing loops, where the line crosses itself in the air as shown. This is a major fault but easily remedied.

The correct position for the commencement of the haul is just after the butt of the rod is vertical.

An exercise to cure tailing loops

If you are still struggling with tailing loops here is an exercise just for you:

Position yourself as though making a forward cast in the vertical plane. Have the line laid out on the grass behind you, feet apart with your body in the same orientation as previously, rod low as shown.

Make one standard forward cast: slow pick up, sharp and fast power snap and the normal follow through, shoot line as you complete the cast and let the line land on the ground. You are again making only one complete stroke at a time. This works because to pick up the slight amount of slack in the line you will find that it is almost impossible to put the power stroke in too early. Repeating this single stroke exercise will help to ingrain the correct position of the rod when making the power stroke. If you are revisiting this exercise, having read the section on hauling, you can add a haul to the forward cast as well.

Other possible problems and their solutions

For a quick reference to problems and their solutions, refer to the problem chart on pages 86 to 88.

Start with the line on the ground behind you and make one single forward cast in the vertical plane.

Watch the line in the air carefully; if it is crossing or getting close to crossing, you are putting in the power stroke too early.

Hauling: turbo-charging your casting

Hauling is an adjunct to a good basic cast. Whilst hauling is a technique that will certainly improve your fishing, it is not a cure for ailing casting technique, and trying to start hauling without having already fully ingrained the basic casting stroke described in the preceding sections will do you more harm than good. There are a number of reasons for this but the most important is that to be able to haul properly, you have to be able to shoot at least some line on both the forward and back cast. So if you have skipped forward (I know that some of you will have done so!), resist the temptation to continue because you are not going to help your cause.

What is hauling?

As we have previously mentioned numerous times, line speed is what makes casting work. Line speed gives you control, distance, accuracy and the ability to dominate even a stiff breeze or turn over a long leader (unfurling the leader completely in the air so it is more or less straight). However, there is a limit to how much line speed you can generate with the basic casting stroke, and hauling is a means of adding more speed during the power stroke without forcing the rod to move in an arc.

Hauling, then, is about using your non-casting hand to pull the line and add speed to the cast.

Learning to haul will increase line speed, accuracy and distance, the latter being an essential element of comfortable and successful stillwater bank fishing.

Two types of haul

There are commonly regarded as being two basic types of haul: the *single haul* and the *double haul*.

Many anglers find themselves making single hauls quite naturally, although usually they make them only on the back cast and this can bring about its own problems. Single hauling is actually not that effective on its own as it tends to feed slack line into the cast, resulting in the loss of power and control.

The most important part of hauling is that when you pull the line in to increase its speed, you have to get rid of it again or you will end up with a heap of line hanging around the handle of your rod and taking all the power from the cast. Most anglers who use a single haul fail to feed out the hauled line, causing this problem, and it is thus best to view single hauling simply as a part of learning to double haul correctly.

Double hauling, as you might imagine, is simply the joining of two single hauls into one: a haul on the back cast followed by a haul on the forward cast. It is one of those things that is complicated to explain and at first confusing to do, but once ingrained you will find yourself doing it in your sleep.

Double hauling is not just about distance

Almost everyone you ask will probably tell you that hauling is a distance casting technique, and that you needn't worry about it if you are only fishing small streams. Certainly, double hauling is not essential to catch fish, even a lot of fish.

What double hauling does do, however, is improve line speed, which in turn improves the cast and allows you to throw narrower loops, longer casts, punch into or across the wind more effectively, gain far greater accuracy, make fewer fish-frightening false casts and reduce the amount of line you need to get airborne to reach any particular target. The last is a very important factor when, as is often the case, there is little if any room behind you to make the back cast.

Double hauling will improve your casting and fishing ability greatly, so long as you have mastered the basic casting stroke first.

Before you set about the exercises in this section answer the following questions:

1. Can you cast good tight loops on both the forward and back casts consistently?
2. Can you shoot a metre or two of line on both the forward and back casts consistently?
3. Can you comfortably cast a distance of between 15 and 20 metres with good form and without hauling?

If you can do all of the above, move onwards. If you can't, then get back out there and practise some more; it will be worth it in the end I PROMISE.

Learning to haul

As with many of the previous exercises you are going to start this one off with the rod horizontal.

Position yourself in the same manner, feet shoulder width apart, rod horizontal to the ground, line held in the non-casting hand and with approximately 10 metres of line out. Make a couple of back and forward casts, letting the line land on the ground, just as you did previously. This should be second nature by now.

Now, starting with the back cast (line in front of you), make the same casting stroke, slow tow-in phase, sharp power stroke and follow through. The only difference is that this time you are going to give the line in your non-casting hand a fairly sudden pull just at the end of the power stroke, by pulling your non-casting hand away from the rod in the position shown below, then let the line land on the grass behind you.

Cast the line back in front of you and let it land on the grass, then repeat the back cast with a haul during the power stroke. You will most likely find it quite difficult to get the pull or haul at exactly the right moment to start with, but persevere.

At this point you are only making one haul at a time and you are *not shooting the line back behind you*. The point is simply to get the timing of the backward haul right.

Before the haul commences both hands are close together.

Here the haul has been added by pulling the line with the non-casting hand. Note that the haul in this picture has been exaggerated for clarity; you need not pull that much line in to achieve results.

Key elements

- Add a haul during the power stroke by pulling the line away from the rod butt during the power snap part of the cast
- Finish the back cast with the non-rod hand farther away from the rod butt than you did previously
- Remember, the haul is added to an already good cast, so maintain the same form, style and tempo that you have already learned. Don't change anything about the basic casting stroke

Problems to watch out for

- Hauling too early: this will generate a tailing loop in the line and it will most likely tangle with itself
- Hauling too late: this will stop the cast and it will go nowhere
- Forgetting the basic casting stroke: if this happens make a few normal casts again before re-attempting the haul

Shooting the line behind you

As mentioned before, the key to hauling effectively is to get rid of the line that you pulled in during the haul. This is done by moving the non-rod hand back towards the rod after the haul, allowing the loop in the line to pull the spare line back out behind you during the follow through.

With the line in front of you, start a normal horizontal back cast: slow tow-in, sharp power snap with a haul of your non-rod hand at the same time, and then once the loop has formed bring your non-rod hand back into position next to the rod to allow the spare line you pulled in to shoot out behind you. Let the line land on the ground as before. On completion of a single back cast, make a normal forward cast to put the line on the grass in front of you and repeat the exercise.

This is a properly executed single haul. Note that there should be no slack left over at the completion of the cast.

Repeat this single haul until you are used to moving your non-rod hand away from the rod butt (the haul) and back again (the shoot). Do not let go of the line; the idea is only to shoot out the line you pulled in, no more.

The basic action here is to move your hands apart and then back together again. You should notice that the loop in the line whilst in the air is even tighter than it was previously and that the line is really singing out, having no trouble at all pulling the slack with it as you shoot.

At the completion of the power stroke, bring your non-casting hand back towards the rod, shooting the line that you have just hauled in back out of the rod tip, ready for the next cast. Note: there is no slack line between the non-casting hand and the rod.

Add the haul late in the power stroke as before.

The complete sequence of the backward haul; again note how the hands move apart during the haul and back together as you shoot the line.

Key elements

- Time the backward haul to coincide with the end of the power snap
- Shoot the line that you pulled in back out again, leaving it straight and taut behind you
- Move the non-rod hand back next to the rod butt after completion of the haul
- Just focus on making one haul and one shoot, then cast the line back to the front and repeat

Problems to watch out for

- Mistiming the haul. If you find this a problem, go back to Exercise 12
- The line not shooting out properly. Check that your basic loop is tight; if not, go back to making a few casts without hauling until you get it right again

Single haul on the forward cast

Having successfully made single hauls on the back cast we will now repeat the process on the forward cast in exactly the same manner. For now, forget about hauling on the back cast and stick to learning one thing at a time. Starting in the same position as previously: rod horizontal with 10 or so metres of line out on the grass, make one or two normal horizontal casts to get the feel of things again.

Leaving the line behind you this time and laying out straight on the grass, make a forward cast but include a haul at the end of the power stroke. Remember still to tow the line in slowly to begin.

This is exactly the same as in Exercise 13 except that we are focusing on the forward cast only.

On the follow through of the forward cast bring your non-casting hand back to its original position, next to the rod butt, so as to shoot the line that you hauled in back out again, and let the line land on the grass in front of you.

Cast the line back behind you in a normal back cast, let the line land on the ground and then repeat the above exercise.

Start this exercise with the line behind you, making a forward cast and haul one stroke at a time. Note the hand position at the start, ready to haul during the power stroke.

Combine a haul with the power stroke, pulling the line late in the power snap.

Shoot the line you hauled in as you follow through and land the line on the ground.

The complete forward haul: tow-in, power snap and haul, shoot line on the follow through.

Key elements

- Time the haul to coincide with the end of the power snap
- Shoot the line out in front of you during the follow through

Problems to watch out for

- Mistiming the haul. Remember to pull the line late in the power snap
- The line not shooting out properly. Practise keeping your loops tight; this should remedy the problem

Double hauling – the 'Holy Grail' of casting

Finally, all that hard work is about to come to fruition. By now you should be making nice, neat casting loops, feeling quite comfortable with your basic casting and adding hauls on both the forward and backward strokes. Now you should be ready for the final step towards being a really great caster.

In this exercise we are going to join those two hauls, both on the forward and back cast, together to create a continuous and stylish casting stroke. As with exercises 13 and 14, make a couple of horizontal casts to get used to the feel of things. The rod position, line, etc. are all exactly the same as with the other exercises.

Make a back cast with a haul (refer to the image of the back haul sequence on page 80) and shoot the line you hauled in back out behind you, letting the line rest on the grass. Make a forward cast with a haul (refer to the image of the foward haul sequence on page 81) and shoot the line you hauled in back out in front of you, again letting the line rest on the grass. Repeat the above sequence as many times as you need to, until you feel quite comfortable with the action and the movement of your hands.

Now do the same thing but don't let the line rest behind you. Simply make a back cast with a haul and shoot, followed by a forward cast with a haul and shoot, letting the line land on the grass in front of you at the completion of each casting cycle.

You are now double hauling. Take things slowly; there is no need to rush it. Keep making one complete casting cycle at a time, until you feel comfortable with the motion. By now you should be feeling the benefits of only adding one element at a time and it shouldn't take too much adjustment to be able to make complete casting strokes one at a time.

Once you have mastered this, repeat the exercise, but this time make two complete casting strokes before you put the line back down on the grass in front of you: slow tow-in backwards, power snap and haul, follow through and shoot spare line, slow tow-in forwards, power snap and haul, follow through and start over again.

When double hauling the most essential element is to shoot out the line that you hauled in before commencing the next casting stroke. Failure to do so is the most common error for beginners trying to learn this technique.

Key elements

- The haul on both the forward and back casts should now be making the loop significantly tighter and the line should be 'pulling' as though it wants to go farther
- Make sure to pull your arms apart (the haul) and bring them together again (the shoot) on each stroke
- Only make one stroke at a time until you are feeling comfortable, then progress gradually to making two complete casting cycles, and then three

Problems to watch out for

- Trying to rush things; every single one of the exercises in this book relies on a foundation of basic casting learned in previous lessons and there is no need to go any faster than you have done with any of the other exercises
- Neglecting the slow tow-in phase at the commencement of each stroke; it may not seem as though this is doing much but it is the foundation of your cast, and you have to start each stroke slowly to get the line moving

Double hauling in the vertical plane

Starting back where you were at the end of Exercise 15, make continuous casting strokes with a haul on both the forward and back casts. Notice the line is now taut all the time throughout the entire cycle; this is what you have been aiming for with all these exercises.

As with Exercise 6 (remember back then when you didn't have a clue? Look how far you have come already!), keeping the casting stroke going, gradually lift the rod from the horizontal to the vertical position. Keep the hauls, the tempo and rhythm all exactly the same; you are merely changing the plane of the cast from the practice position to the actual vertical casting stroke that you will use for most of your fishing.

Congratulations, you should now be making double haul casts like a pro. This is the time to practise some more in the overhead position until you get things really smooth. If at any time things start to go wrong go back to the relevant horizontal exercise and repeat it; this is the foundation of getting your casting to be truly spectacular. Once you can make vertical casts with a double haul as shown, you are ready to take on almost any casting situation with confidence and style.

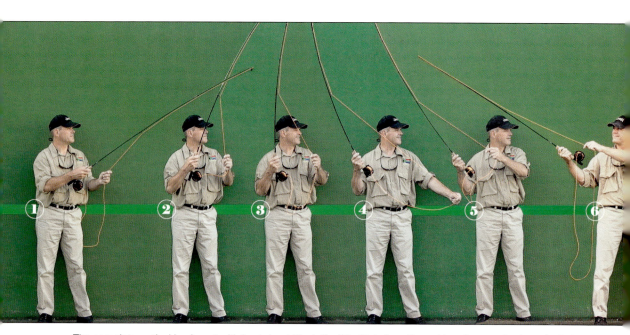

The complete vertical back cast with haul should look like this. Note how the rod hand moves backwards during the power snap to provide the necessary straight movement of the rod tip.

Even great casters practise some of the time, so be proud of what you have achieved. If you can make double haul casts at will, you are amongst the top 20% of fly-casters in the world and you are going to enjoy your fishing a lot more than you ever did, without having to worry about the mechanics of it all. Now you can focus on fishing, which was after all the point of the exercise in the first place!

Finally, whilst repeating this exercise, let the line slip through an 'O' in your fingers on the final delivery; you will be quite amazed at how much line will be pulled out. You have now reached the zenith of fly-casting and all that is left to be done is to go fishing (and perhaps do some more practice now and then to further hone your newly acquired skills).

The complete vertical forward cast with haul should look like this. Note how the rod hand moves forwards during the power snap to provide the necessary straight movement of the rod tip.

Further practice exercises

Fly-casting, especially now that you are getting the hang of things, can be fun just for its own sake. Even if you can't go fishing, at least you can find an hour or two once in a while to have a practice. The following are exercises that you can try out to further improve your effectiveness and confidence. These are more like casting games really; just remember that you can always go back to the learning process at any point if you find things are going wrong. Some of the following exercises are particularly geared towards preparing you to take what you have learned and apply it to actual fishing. Enjoy the process; you have done all the hard work and you should be able to see clearly the benefits of your diligence.

Improving control: Making deliberate tight and open loops

In the horizontal practice position, make multiple casts, trying deliberately to make some wide and some narrow casting loops. Although for the most part you will want tight loops, this exercise will increase the control you have over your rod and line. Have fun with this exercise; it is merely some advanced practice to help you get even better.

Improving accuracy: Aiming at targets

When you are actually fishing, the targets, whether fish or at least places where you expect there to be fish, will vary constantly as to their position and distance from you.

With a small piece of wool on the end of the leader acting as a fly, make casts at a range of targets (plates, hula hoops, etc.) scattered around you at random. Move about so as to change constantly the angle and distance, and remember that in real fishing situations the distance cast is as important as the direction, so focus on both.

This can be a fun way to improve your casting accuracy; you will be surprised how accurately your brain can calculate the distances after a bit of practice. This exercise is the closest thing to fishing that you can achieve without actually being on the water.

Reducing false casts

Try the same exercise as above, but limit yourself to only two false casts. With a bit of practice you will quickly become surprised how much distance can be covered by shooting line without lots of false casting.

Improving line control

Make long casts on the grass, and practise putting the line in your non-casting hand over the fulcrum of the index finger of your casting hand without looking down. Pull in some line and re-cast, repeating the exercise. With a bit of practice you will be able to do this without having to look down. This will pay big dividends when you are actually fishing and a fish takes; if you are looking down you are going to miss the fish. Of course, you can combine this exercise with almost all of the others so that you can practise two different things at once.

Casting at targets placed at different distances and angles will help prepare you for actual fishing situations.

Casting into the wind

When you are out practising, have a go at turning around and casting into the wind. Whilst it is true that nobody can really cast quite as well or as far into a stiff breeze as they can with the wind behind them, it is more than possible to cast plenty far enough even into a minor gale.

The trick to casting effectively into the wind is not necessarily to add more power but rather just to keep a tight loop and aim a little downwards in order to land the line quickly on the ground, so that it doesn't blow back at you. You will soon gain the confidence that a windy day need not stop you fishing.

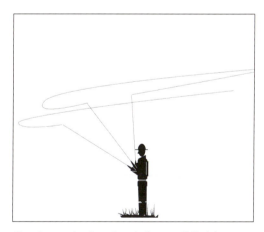

Practise casting into the wind; you will find that casting slightly downwards on the forward stroke, as in the image, will assist in stopping the line blowing back into your face.

Casting back-hand

Practise making your final delivery behind you instead of in front of you. This may seem a little odd but there are times (like when the wind is blowing a gale over your casting shoulder) when backhand casting can mean the difference between catching fish and going home with a hook in your ear. Just set up your position so that the targets are behind you and cast away.

Become ambidextrous

Go through the exercises in this book using your other hand to make the casts. This is not strictly necessary but it can be fun and will impress your mates no end. It may take a little longer to educate your non-dominant hand but the step-by-step process will work in exactly the same manner.

Good casting and line control can put your fly into places that other anglers cannot reach.

Practise casting under obstructions

By now you should be well aware that casting a tight loop has all manner of advantages, not the least of which is the ability to cast under trees and bank-side vegetation.

Hang a tyre or hula-hoop in a tree and cast the line through it, and practise casting under fences or bushes.

Casting distance

OK, this is the one that everybody wants to do but beware; it can spoil your casting if you become hung up on it. In all likelihood the temptation will immediately be to overpower the cast, start your power stroke too early and ruin all the hard work you've done. The only advantage is that now you will be able to go back and refocus if you need to.

Making normal overhead casts with all the fly-line off the reel and lying on the ground at your feet ready to shoot, complete one or two casting cycles and then shoot as much line as possible.

Resist the temptation to give the final cast a huge swipe; it doesn't work and you should know that by now. Pace out the distance and try to improve on it as time goes on. Remember, though, that a well-formed cast is better than having the line land in a heap, no matter how far it goes.

Being able to cast a full fly-line is both satisfying and useful, but don't get hung up on it.

Finally

I hope that you have benefited from going through the exercises in this book and that by now you have total confidence in your casting.

It isn't something that most authors would say, but I honestly hope that you forget you ever read this book; great fly-casting is about being able to go fishing without ever thinking about the mechanics.

One day, out on a stream, in a boat or casting on a bonefish flat somewhere, I hope that you will spare no thought for this book, all the exercises and the time you spent out on the lawn.

Forgetting that you ever 'Learn(ed) to Fly-cast in a Weekend' would be the sincerest form of flattery, because it would mean that I have achieved what I set out to do in this book. So, in closing, I wish you tight lines, great fishing and most of all lots and lots of fun, because fly-fishing isn't really about casting at all, it is about enjoying yourself, and by now I trust that you are better equipped to do that.

Tim Rolston
Cape Town
2007

Appendix

QUICK REFERENCE TO FAULTFINDING AND CURES		
Problem	**Probable Cause**	**Solution**
My casts lack power, the loop is wide and the line fails to straighten out either in front or behind me.	There is no distinct power snap in the cast; the casting speed is too much the same throughout.	Go back to Exercise 2. Changing speeds and making one stroke at a time, focus on the short sharp power snap on every cast. Make sure this occurs on both the forward and back casts. Keep them separate until you have the movement ingrained.
When I commence a vertical cast with the line on the ground in front of me, the first stroke lacks power and the line fails to form a neat loop on the back cast.	Most likely you are holding the rod tip too high when you commence the cast.	Lower the rod tip before you start the cast and pull in the slack line before you make the first back stroke.
When shooting line, what was previously a good cast with a tight loop fails and all power is lost.	Most likely you are letting the line go at the wrong moment, You have to hold the line tight until the loop has formed. Letting line go before that means that the power snap has nothing to pull against. Listen for line sliding through the rings during the power snap. This is a dead giveaway that you have let go too early.	Go back to Exercise 8 and practise shooting line on the horizontal plane.
When shooting line the line bounces back towards me and goes nowhere.	You are letting go of the line with your non-casting hand too late. The loop has formed and is trying to pull line with it but you are still holding onto it.	Go back to Exercise 8, and practise the timing. Remember to let go of the line the moment the loop has been formed.
My line tangles around itself in the air.	You are throwing 'tailing loops'.	Check out the remedial steps for tailing loops in Exercise 11.

Problem	Probable Cause	Solution
When making casts the line 'kicks' around at the end of the stroke.	This isn't a bad fault; it actually means that you have a good tight loop carrying lots of momentum. Most likely you don't have a leader on the line. Leaders slow the line down at the end of the cast, so when you are actually fishing you will probably never experience this problem.	Add a leader to the end of your line, or even add a small tuft of wool to the end of the leader. This should 'cure' what isn't really a fault in your casting stroke.
When making vertical casts my line keeps hitting the ground behind me.	You are either: 1) Not commencing the forward stroke early enough. 2) Casting downwards behind you by making the power stroke at an angle to the ground. 3) Tipping the rod in a severe arc on the back cast.	1) Start the forward cast just before the line straightens. 2) Keep the power stroke slightly 'up hill' on the back. 3) Your shoulder may be in the way forcing you to 'break your wrist' during the power stroke. Check that you are at an angle to the direction of the cast and keep your shoulder out of the way.
The line keeps hitting me when I make the forward cast.	Most likely you are casting with a breeze coming over your casting shoulder, blowing the line into you as you come forward.	If you are just practising you can simply move position relative to the wind. If you are fishing and there are no other options you will just have to deal with it.
I am double hauling but my forward cast is poor compared to my back cast.	This is very common and simply because you are not shooting the slack line behind you when making the back cast, putting slack into the line and leaving nothing to 'pull against' as you commence the forward stroke.	Go back to the horizontal exercises on hauling; focus on shooting the line behind you when you make the back cast. To start with, let the line land on the ground each time until you have ingrained the behaviour of shooting out the line.

Problem	Probable Cause	Solution
I am single hauling and my forward cast is poor.	You are single hauling on the backstroke. If you wish to single haul then only haul on the final forward stroke and let the line go.	Single hauling is not particularly effective and worse than useless if you haul on the back stroke only. Revisit the exercises on horizontal casting with hauls.
My arms are getting tired.	The most likely reason for this is 'reaching'; that is holding the rod up and a long way from your body. Beginners seem to want to do this all the time, and although it doesn't badly affect your casting it will make you tired.	Check the various images in this book and look at the position of the caster's elbow. It should be comfortably hanging close to the body at just above waist height and relaxed.
Every time I start a new exercise my casting gets worse.	Again this is normal; adding an extra element can 'confuse' your muscles. This is why we are only adding one new thing at a time.	Simply go back to the previous exercise and ingrain the movements again before moving on.
The line unfurls off vertical as I make the final cast.	The variation between the line of the back cast and the forward cast is too large.	Most casters make the two strokes in slightly different planes but if it is too excessive the line will unfurl in an odd shape. Focus on keeping the rod more in the same plane on the forward and back casts.
The line 'ploughs' into the ground in front of me.	Your power stroke is tipped downwards from vertical.	Try to keep the power stroke either perpendicular with the ground or on a slight upward slope as you make it.
My wife is casting much better than I am and she only started yesterday.	Your good lady is not trying to use power and is relying on good form.	Avoid the tendency to use more force, relax and if necessary go back to the first couple of exercises again, working your way through them and avoiding trying too hard.

Outfit weights and applications

The table below should offer novices some idea of the purposes of various AFTMA line and rod weight fly-fishing gear. It is meant as a guideline for relative beginners only. There are plenty of exceptions, what with anglers catching bonefish on #2 weight gear and such, but if you are choosing tackle it should offer some assistance.

AFTMA Line and Rod	Suitable Types of Fishing	Advantages	Disadvantages
'0' to '3' weight	Small stream trout fishing, particularly with dry flies or light nymphs and emergers.	Very accurate short-range casting and light presentation of the fly. Particularly suited to short-range pocket water fishing. Protects against breakage of fine tippets.	Will not cast well at long range. Lacks power to hook fish at long range. Lacks power to fight really large fish. Will not cast large or heavy flies. Available line types limited. Very specialised; not suitable as a 'general purpose outfit'.
'4' to '6' weight	General stream and lightweight stillwater trout fishing. Also suitable for yellowfish and other species up to about 4 kg and small-lure bass and panfish fishing.	Highly adaptable to a variety of fishing applications. Very wide range of different line types available. Great general purpose or travel rods.	Cast better at mid-range than very close. Do not offer the same tippet protection as the ultra-light gear. Still will not allow fishing with very large or heavy flies. Not suitable for small streams.
'7' to '8' weight	Suitable for light estuary fishing, bonefish flats, competition boat angling for trout, sea trout fishing and fishing large rivers with big or heavy flies. Also for casting large 'bass bugs' for black bass.	Additional power allows the fishing of large and heavy flies. Will cast large patterns even in a stiff breeze. Plenty of backbone to fight larger and faster kinds of fish.	Cannot be fished effectively on small streams. Delicacy of presentation starts to suffer. Will not protect light tippets much. Will 'outgun' smaller fish and remove the challenge of fishing.

AFTMA Line and Rod	Suitable Types of Fishing	Advantages	Disadvantages
'9' to '10' weight	Suitable for salmon on medium to large rivers and the mainstay gear for the saltwater angler fishing estuaries or into the surf. Also for Tiger fish and other large predatory species where big flies are required.	Capable of casting long distances with large or heavy fly patterns. Wide range of line types available. Powerful enough to land large fish.	Virtually unusable for trout fishing. Far too heavy for even large trout streams and lakes. Difficult to achieve casting delicacy. Will not protect light tippets well. Will prove tiring to use without good technique. Most rods in these weights will require double haul technique to make them work well. Useless for short-range accurate casting. Not suitable as a 'general purpose outfit'.
'11' to '12' weight	Specialist rods: either double-handed salmon fishing gear or single-handed boat fishing gear. Suitable for heavy gear saltwater fishing, giant kingfish, dorado, tarpon, etc. with large, air-resistant or heavy flies.	Will allow casting of huge baitfish-style flies. Will overcome substantial wind without effort. Powerhouse gear for large fish and large flies.	Very limited in terms of presentation delicacy. Suitable only for fishing large flies. Line types available still somewhat limited. Tiring to cast all day without very good technique. Very poor protection of light tippets. Not suitable as a 'general purpose outfit'.
'13' to '15' weight	Very much specialist gear for massive salt-water fish when boat fishing. These are 'fish-fighting' rods rather than 'casting' rods.	Mostly used for saltwater boat fishing for large predatory fish, giant trevally, sailfish, tuna and marlin. Lack stylish casting ability, but have massive amounts of power to fight and 'lift' large fish.	Casting delicacy non-existent. Tippet protection severely limited. Available line types very limited. Unsuitable for most other types of fly-fishing.

Glossary of fly-fishing and fly-casting terminology

AFTMA	American Fishing Tackle Manufacturers Association.
AFTMA number	A designation of the weight of the fly-line and corresponding suitable rod, usually denoted by a # symbol.
Arbour	The drum of the fly-fishing reel, usually used when referring to large arbour reels.
Back cast	That portion of the casting stroke that throws the line behind the angler.
Backing	Non-stretch (usually Dacron or similar, or Kevlar) cord attached between the fly-line and the reel, allowing the fish to run much farther than the length of the fly-line when hooked.
Braided core	The centre of fly-lines, made out of braided material.
Braided loop	A form of connector made of braided nylon and used to connect the leader to the fly-line.
Breaking the wrist	The action of extreme extension of the angle between the wrist and the forearm during casting.
Carbon fibre	Carbon strands used together with resins to build most modern fly-rods.
Cast (1)	The action of throwing the fly or lure using the weight of the line to do so.
Cast (2)	An English term for the leader, not used much these days.
Casting hand	The hand used to hold the rod whilst casting.
Clock system	A method of describing the action of the rod during a cast and using the position of the clock hands to indicate where to apply power or stop; extremely misleading and inaccurate manner of describing the actual action of fly-casting.
Cork	The preferred material for the manufacture of fly-fishing rod handles, it offers good grip and comfort; all quality fly-fishing rods use cork as a handle material although the quality does vary.
Drag (1)	The resistance on the line applied by a braking mechanism in the reel.

Drag (2)	The movement of a fly on or in the water in an unnatural manner, that is at a different speed to the water.
Eyes	See Snake guide and Single foot guide.
False cast	Making a casting stroke in the air without putting the line on the water; usually used to let out more line or change direction of the cast before making the final delivery.
Fast action rods	Rods with a rapid recovery from flexing as when casting.
Flex rating	A designation used by some rod manufacturers to indicate the 'stiffness' of a fly-rod, or the speed with which it recovers from being flexed, as during casting.
Floating line	A fly-line designed to be less dense than water, such that it will float.
Fly	A lure, representing an insect or baitfish, usually hand tied with feathers, fur and synthetic materials.
Fly-line	Specifically manufactured and normally tapered line, previously of silk but now of plastic-coated core.
Forward cast	That portion of the casting stroke that throws the line in front of the angler.
Grip (1)	The form of the casting hand around the handle. It is recommended that you grip the rod with the thumb opposite the reel at all times.
Grip (2)	Some, particularly American, writers use the term 'grip' as an alternative to the 'rod handle'.
Haul	The action of using the non-casting hand to pull line at the appropriate point in the cast to increase line speed.
Haul (double)	The action of using the non-casting hand to pull the line to increase line speed on both the back and forward casting strokes.
Haul (single)	The action of using the non-casting hand to pull line at the appropriate point in the cast but in one direction only.
Hook (n)	The fishing hook onto which the fly or lure is tied during manufacture.
Hook (v)	The action of striking and catching the fish's mouth with the hook portion of the fly.
Hook keeper	A tiny ring fitted to some rods just above the handle to store the fly when not in use.

Intermediate line	A fly-line designed to be only slightly denser than water, such that it sinks very slowly.
Large arbour reel	A reel with a specifically designed wide and large diameter spool to reduce line kink and lessen the increase in resistance as line is paid out from the reel.
Leader	Portion of either level, tapered or sectional nylon monofilament or fluorocarbon, acting as a link between the fly-line and the fly.
Loop	The shape of the line as it unfolds in the air, rather like the tracks of a tank. Narrow loops are indicators of good casting technique.
Mono core	The centre of fly-lines, made out of nylon monofilament.
Nail knot	A knot specifically used to connect the leader to the fly-line; usually tied using a nail or needle.
Non-casting hand	The hand used to manipulate the line whilst casting; also usually the hand used for manipulating the reel.
Overhead cast	The basic fly-casting style; there are many others with specific applications, roll-casting, spey-casting, etc.
Overloading	The practice of using lines with an AFTMA number higher than the rod to which they are fitted.
Power snap	The short sharp acceleration of the rod tip during the casting stroke; this forms the loop of the cast.
Reel	A winch fitted to the base of the rod to hold the line and allow line to pay out smoothly when playing a fish.
Reel seat	A fitting at the base of the rod handle used to attach the reel.
Retrieve	The action of pulling in line, either to move the fly in a natural or enticing manner or simply to take up slack as the line moves towards the angler, as in fishing on a stream.
Rod butt	The terminal end of a fly-rod, usually referring to the last section of the handle but sometimes also the final section of the rod blank above the handle.
Rod tip	The very tip of the rod; it is the movement of the tip of the rod that will determine the shape of the loop and the quality of the cast.
Running line	Portion of a fly-line not designed to be cast but only 'shot' out at the end of the final casting stroke; usually thinner than the main line to reduce friction with rod and air.

Shooting line (n)	See running line.
Shooting line (v)	The action of releasing line to be carried out and away from the rod under the influence of the front portion of the line.
Single foot guide	A rod ring with a single foot and usually circular; easier to manufacture and reduced rod weight but generally regarded as offering more friction than snake guides do.
Sinking line	A fly-line designed to be denser than water such that it will sink, generally of dark colour and not ideal to use when practising casting, being too difficult to see.
Slow action rods	Rods with a less rapid recovery from flexing when casting.
Snake guide	A rod ring formed in an open spiral, providing little friction to the line during casting, but adding weight to the rod and increasing manufacturing time and cost.
Snap	An alternative term for the power stroke during the cast.
Stance	The position of the angler whilst casting.
Stripping guide	The final one or two guides on a fly-rod just above the handle, usually lined to reduce wear and large to allow reduced friction when casting.
Stroke	That portion of a fly cast, usually referring to the forward or backward stroke forming the forward or back cast respectively.
Tailing loop	A cast loop that crosses itself in the air, usually resulting in a tangle; indication of poor style.
Taper (fly-line)	The shape of the fly-line, generally double taper (with the same taper at either end) or weight forward taper (with a casting taper at the front and shooting or running line at the rear).
Tippet	The final and usually the thinnest portion of nylon monofilament or fluorocarbon in the leader.
Tip top guide	The final guide at the very tip of the rod.
Tow-in phase	That portion of the casting stroke when starting the cast or changing direction where the line is moved slowly to commence the casting stroke.
Wind knot	An overhand knot formed in the fly-line or leader that is caused by casting a tailing loop and not actually by the wind.

Index

Page references in italics refer to photographs or diagrams.

Catch and release

Learning to fly-cast is but one of many facets of becoming a better angler; however, with increased fishing effectiveness comes added responsibility. Certainly I hope that learning to cast well will go a long way to improving your enjoyment of fly-fishing as well as your catch rate, but do bear in mind that this planet is a rare and wonderful jewel, that its resources are finite, and that generations to come have to live with what we leave for them. Your children's and grandchildren's opportunities to enjoy the pleasures of fishing are dependent on us all acting responsibly. No matter what species you target, practise catch and release as far as the rules allow. Show respect for your quarry; use barbless hooks, handle the fish with care and release them back into the environment for the benefit of future generations of both people and fish.